Born in Ireland in 1898, C. S. Lewis was educated at Malvern College for a year and then privately. He gained a triple First at Oxford and was a Fellow and Tutor at Magdalen College 1925-54. In 1954 he became Professor of Mediaeval and Renaissance Literature at Cambridge. He was an outstanding and popular lecturer and had a lasting influence on his pupils.

C. S. Lewis was for many years an atheist, and described his conversion in *Surprised by Joy*: 'In the Trinity term of 1929 I gave in, and admitted that God was God . . . perhaps the most dejected and reluctant convert in all England.' It was this experience that helped him to understand not only apathy but active unwillingness to accept religion, and, as a Christian writer gifted with an exceptionally brilliant and logical mind and a lucid, lively style, he was without peer. *The Problem of Pain, The Screwtape Letters, Mere Christianity, The Four Loves* and the posthumous *Prayer: Letters to Malcolm* are only a few of his best-selling works. He also wrote some delightful books for children and some science fiction, besides many works of literary criticism. His works are known to millions of people all over the world in translation. He died on 22 November 1963, at his home in Oxford.

FERN-SEED
AND ELEPHANTS
and other essays on Christianity
by C. S. Lewis

Edited by Walter Hooper

Collins/Fountain Books
A Fontana Series

This collection first issued in Fontana 1975
Second Impression May 1976
Reprinted in Fountain Books February 1977

© The Trustees of the Estate of C. S. Lewis 1975

Made and printed in Great Britain by
William Collins Sons & Co Ltd, Glasgow

CONTENTS

PREFACE

Professor Tolkien once teased me about C. S. Lewis being the only one of his friends who had published more books *after* his death than before. He had in his hands at that moment the seventh volume of Lewis's writings which I had edited. What might seem to have been overzealousness on my own part to get those writings into print will probably not be thought so when the reader knows that many hundreds of letters regularly cross my desk asking for yet 'another Lewis book' and that the sales of Lewis's works have more than trebled since his death in 1963.

There is an enthusiastic revival of interest in Lewis. Not only are the sales of his books steadily increasing everywhere, but there are clubs devoted to the study of his work, and I hear almost every week of some American university which, moved by popular demand, has added to its syllabus a course on Lewis's thought. But 'revival' is not perhaps the right word because, though there was a momentary shifting of interest in the 1960s when we were inundated by the theological novelties of the liberals, Lewis's books never ceased being popular. I think the recent upsurge of interest in Lewis is partially attributable to a sound, growing and unstoppable interest in Christianity itself. But only partially. Lewis's genuine and enduring value – that which continues to endear him to a growing number of readers – lies in his ability not only to do combat but to cleanse: to provide for the mind an authentic vision of the Faith which purges and replaces error, uncertainty and especially the presumptuousness of those who, as Lewis says in this book, 'claim to see fern-seed and can't see an elephant ten yards away in broad daylight'.

All but one of these essays have been published before, but as they have been out of print for some time, and as two (5 and 7) have never before now appeared in this country, they will be new to most readers. (1) 'Membership' was read to the Society of St Alban and St Sergius, Oxford, and published in *Sobornost*, No. 31 (June 1945) and afterwards in Lewis's *Transposition and Other Addresses* (1949). (2) 'Learning in War-Time' was preached in the Church of St Mary the Virgin, Oxford, on 22 October 1939, and published in *Transposition and Other Addresses*. (3) The manuscript of 'On Forgiveness' came to light while this book was in preparation. The essay was written in 1947 and has never been published anywhere before. (4) 'Historicism' was written for, and published in, *The Month*, IV (Oct. 1950) and was reprinted in Lewis's *Christian Reflections* (1967). (5) 'The World's Last Night' was published first under the title 'Christian Hope – Its Meaning for Today' in *Religion in Life*, XXI (Winter 1951–52), and later under its new title in Lewis's *The World's Last Night and Other Essays* (New York, 1960). (6) 'Religion and Rocketry' was published as 'Will We Lose God in Outer Space?' in *Christian Herald*, LXXXI (April 1958), as a pamphlet entitled *Shall We Lose God in Outer Space?* by S.P.C.K. in 1959 and afterwards under the only title Lewis gave it – 'Religion and

Rocketry' – in *The World's Last Night*. (7) 'The Efficacy of Prayer' appeared first in *The Atlantic Monthly*, CCIII (Jan. 1959) and afterwards in *The World's Last Night*. (8) 'Fern-seed and Elephants' was read to the students of Westcott House, a theological college at Cambridge, on 11 May 1959, and was published under the title 'Modern Theology and Biblical Criticism' in *Christian Reflections*. Austin Farrer told me he thought it the best thing Lewis ever wrote and it has continued to draw astonished admiration from Christians everywhere who see it as – if there can be such a thing – the 'last word' in answer to the demythologizers. My friend, Lady Collins, urged me to find an eye-catching title for this collection, and as I had never been particularly happy about my original name for this last essay, I looked for, and discovered within its pages, a title which I think Lewis might himself have chosen.

Oxford   WALTER HOOPER

MEMBERSHIP

No Christian and, indeed, no historian could accept the epigram which defines religion as 'what a man does with his solitude'. It was one of the Wesleys, I think, who said that the New Testament knows nothing of solitary religion. We are forbidden to neglect the assembling of ourselves together. Christianity is already institutional in the earliest of its documents. The Church is the Bride of Christ. We are members of one another.

In our own age the idea that religion belongs to our private life – that it is, in fact, an occupation for the individual's hour of leisure – is at once paradoxical, dangerous, and natural. It is paradoxical because this exaltation of the individual in the religious field springs up in an age when collectivism is ruthlessly defeating the individual in every other field. I see this even in a university. When I first went to Oxford the typical undergraduate society consisted of a dozen men, who knew one another intimately, hearing a paper by one of their own number in a small sitting-room and hammering out their problem till one or two in the morning. Before the war the typical undergraduate society had come to be a mixed audience of one or two hundred students assembled in a public hall to hear a lecture from some visiting celebrity. Even on those rare occasions when a modern undergraduate is not attending some such society he is seldom engaged

in those solitary walks, or walks with a single
companion, which built the minds of the previous
generations. He lives in a crowd; caucus has replaced
friendship. And this tendency not only exists both
within and without the university, but is often
approved. There is a crowd of busybodies, self-
appointed masters of ceremonies, whose life is devoted
to destroying solitude wherever solitude still exists.
They call it 'taking the young people out of themselves', or 'waking them up', or 'overcoming their
apathy'. If an Augustine, a Vaughan, a Traherne or a
Wordsworth should be born in the modern world, the
leaders of a youth organization would soon cure him.
If a really good home, such as the home of Alcinous
and Arete in the *Odyssey* or the Rostovs in *War
and Peace* or any of Charlotte M. Yonge's families,
existed today, it would be denounced as *bourgeois* and
every engine of destruction would be levelled against it.
And even where the planners fail and someone is left
physically by himself, the wireless has seen to it that
he will be – in a sense not intended by Scipio – never
less alone than when alone. We live, in fact, in a
world starved for solitude, silence, and privacy: and
therefore starved for meditation and true friendship.

That religion should be relegated to solitude in such
an age is, then, paradoxical. But it is also dangerous
for two reasons. In the first place, when the modern
world says to us aloud, 'You may be religious when
you are alone', it adds under its breath, 'and I will see
to it that you never are alone.' To make Christianity
a private affair while banishing all privacy is to relegate
it to the rainbow's end or the Greek calends. That is

one of the enemy's stratagems. In the second place, there is the danger that real Christians who know that Christianity is not a solitary affair may react against that error by simply transporting into our spiritual life that same collectivism which has already conquered our secular life. That is the enemy's other stratagem. Like a good chess player he is always trying to manœuvre you into a position where you can save your castle only by losing your bishop. In order to avoid the trap we must insist that though the private conception of Christianity is an error it is a profoundly natural one, and is clumsily attempting to guard a great truth. Behind it is the obvious feeling that our modern collectivism is an outrage upon human nature and that from this, as from all other evils, God will be our shield and buckler.

This feeling is just. As personal and private life is lower than participation in the Body of Christ, so the collective life is lower than the personal and private life and has no value save in its service. The secular community, since it exists for our natural good and not for our supernatural, has no higher end than to facilitate and safeguard the family, and friendship, and solitude. To be happy at home, said Johnson, is the end of all human endeavour. As long as we are thinking only of natural values we must say that the sun looks down on nothing half so good as a household laughing together over a meal, or two friends talking over a pint of beer, or a man alone reading a book that interests him; and that all economics, politics, laws, armies, and institutions, save in so far as they prolong and multiply such scenes, are a mere plough-

ing the sand and sowing the ocean, a meaningless
vanity and vexation of spirit. Collective activities are,
of course, necessary; but this is the end to which they
are necessary. Great sacrifices of this private happiness
by those who have it may be necessary in order that
it may be more widely distributed. All may have to be
a little hungry in order that none may starve. But do
not let us mistake necessary evils for good. The mistake
is easily made. Fruit has to be tinned if it is to be
transported, and has to lose thereby some of its good
qualities. But one meets people who have learned
actually to prefer the tinned fruit to the fresh. A sick
society must think much about politics, as a sick man
must think much about his digestion: to ignore the
subject may be fatal cowardice for the one as for the
other. But if either comes to regard it as the natural
food of the mind – if either forgets that we think of
such things only in order to be able to think of something else – then what was undertaken for the sake of
health has become itself a new and deadly disease.

There is, in fact, a fatal tendency in all human
activities for the means to encroach upon the very ends
which they were intended to serve. Thus money comes
to hinder the exchange of commodities, and rules of
art to hamper genius, and examinations to prevent
young men from becoming learned. It does not, unfortunately, always follow that the encroaching means
can be dispensed with. I think it probable that the
collectivism of our life is necessary and will increase;
and I think that our only safeguard against its deathly
properties is in a Christian life; for we were promised
that we could handle serpents and drink deadly things

and yet live. That is the truth behind the erroneous definition of religion with which we started. Where it went wrong was in opposing to the collective mass mere solitude. The Christian is called, not to individualism but to membership in the mystical body. A consideration of the differences between the secular collective and the mystical body is therefore the first step to understanding how Christianity without being individualistic can yet counteract collectivism.

At the outset we are hampered by a difficulty of language. The very word *membership* is of Christian origin, but it has been taken over by the world and emptied of all meaning. In any book on logic you may see the expression 'members of a class'. It must be most emphatically stated that the items or particulars included in a homogeneous class are almost the reverse of what St Paul meant by *members*. By *members* (μέλη) he meant what we should call *organs*, things essentially different from, and complementary to, one another: things differing not only in structure and function but also in dignity. Thus, in a club, the committee as a whole, and the servants as a whole, may both properly be regarded as 'members'; what we should call the members of the club are merely units. A row of identically dressed and identically trained soldiers set side by side, or a number of citizens listed as voters in a constituency, are not members of anything in the Pauline sense. I am afraid that when we describe a man as 'a member of the Church' we usually mean nothing Pauline: we mean only that he is a unit – that he is one more specimen of some kind of things as X and Y and Z. How true membership in a body differs from inclusion in a collective may be seen in the structure of a family. The grandfather, the parents, the grown-up son, the child, the dog, and the cat are true members (in the organic sense) precisely because they are not members or units of a homogeneous class. They are not interchangeable. Each person is almost a species in himself. The mother is not simply a different person from the daughter, she is a different kind of person. The grown-up brother is not simply one unit in the class children, he is a separate estate of the realm. The father and grandfather are almost as different as the cat and the dog. If you subtract any one member you have not simply reduced the family in number, you have inflicted an injury on its structure. Its unity is a unity of unlikes, almost of incommensurables.

A dim perception of the richness inherent in this kind of unity is one reason why we enjoy a book like *The Wind in the Willows*; a trio such as Rat, Mole, and Badger symbolizes the extreme differentiation of persons in harmonious union which we know intuitively to be our true refuge both from solitude and from the collective. The affection between such oddly matched couples as Dick Swiveller and the Marchioness, or Mr Pickwick and Sam Weller, pleases in the same way. That is why the modern notion that children should call their parents by their Christian names is so perverse. For this is an effort to ignore the difference in kind which makes for real organic unity. They are trying to inoculate the child with the preposterous view that one's mother is simply a fellow-citizen like anyone else, to make it ignorant of what

all men know and insensible to what all men feel.
They are trying to drag the featureless repetitions of
the collective into the fuller and more concrete world
of the family.

A convict has a number instead of a name. That is
the collective idea carried to its extreme. But a man
in his own house may also lose his name, because he
is called simply 'Father'. That is membership in a
body. The loss of the name in both cases reminds us
that there are two opposite ways of departing from
isolation.

The society into which the Christian is called at
baptism is not a collective but a Body. It is in fact
that Body of which the family is an image on the
natural level. If anyone came to it with the mis-
conception that membership of the Church was
membership in a debased modern sense – a massing
together of persons as if they were pennies or counters
– he would be corrected at the threshold by the
discovery that the head of this Body is so unlike the
inferior members that they share no predicate with
him save by analogy. We are summoned from the
outset to combine as creatures with our Creator, as
mortals with immortal, as redeemed sinners with sin-
less Redeemer. His presence, the interaction between
him and us, must always be the overwhelmingly
dominant factor in the life we are to lead within the
Body; and any conception of Christian fellowship
which does not mean primarily fellowship with him is
out of court. After that it seems almost trivial to trace
further down the diversity of operations to the unity
of the Spirit. But it is very plainly there. There are

priests divided from the laity, catechumens divided from those who are in full fellowship. There is authority of husbands over wives and parents over children. There is, in forms too subtle for official embodiment, a continual interchange of complementary ministrations. We are all constantly teaching and learning, forgiving and being forgiven, representing Christ to man when we intercede, and man to Christ when others intercede for us. The sacrifice of selfish privacy which is daily demanded of us is daily repaid a hundredfold in the true growth of personality which the life of the Body encourages. Those who are members of one another become as diverse as the hand and the ear. That is why the worldlings are so monotonously alike compared with the almost fantastic variety of the saints. Obedience is the road to freedom, humility the road to pleasure, unity the road to personality.

And now I must say something that may appear to you a paradox. You have often heard that, though in the world we hold different stations, yet we are all equal in the sight of God. There are of course senses in which this is true. God is no accepter of persons: his love for us is not measured by our social rank or our intellectual talents. But I believe there is a sense in which this maxim is the reverse of the truth. I am going to venture to say that artificial equality is necessary in the life of the State, but that in the Church we strip off this disguise, we recover our real inequalities, and are thereby refreshed and quickened.

I believe in political equality. But there are two opposite reasons for being a democrat. You may think

18

all men so good that they deserve a share in the government of the commonwealth, and so wise that the commonwealth needs their advice. That is, in my opinion, the false, romantic doctrine of democracy. On the other hand, you may believe fallen men to be so wicked that not one of them can be trusted with any irresponsible power over his fellows.

That I believe to be the true ground of democracy. I do not believe that God created an egalitarian world. I believe the authority of parent over child, husband over wife, learned over simple, to have been as much a part of the original plan as the authority of man over beast. I believe that if we had not fallen Filmer would be right, and patriarchal monarchy would be the sole lawful government. But since we have learned sin, we have found, as Lord Acton says, that 'all power corrupts, and absolute power corrupts absolutely.' The only remedy has been to take away the powers and substitute a legal fiction of equality. The authority of father and husband has been rightly abolished on the legal plane, not because this authority is in itself bad (on the contrary, it is, I hold, divine in origin) but because fathers and husbands are bad. Theocracy has been rightly abolished not because it is bad that learned priests should govern ignorant laymen, but because priests are wicked men like the rest of us. Even the authority of man over beast has had to be interfered with because it is constantly abused.

Equality is for me in the same position as clothes. It is a result of the Fall and the remedy for it. Any attempt to retrace the steps by which we have arrived at egalitarianism and to re-introduce the old authorities on the political level is for me as foolish as it would be to take off our clothes. The Nazi and the nudist make the same mistake. But it is the naked body, still there beneath the clothes of each one of us, which really lives. It is the hierarchical world, still alive and (very properly) hidden behind a façade of equal citizenship, which is our real concern.

Do not misunderstand me. I am not in the least belittling the value of this egalitarian fiction which is our only defence against one another's cruelty. I should view with the strongest disapproval any proposal to abolish manhood suffrage, or the Married Women's Property Act. But the function of equality is purely protective. It is medicine, not food. By treating human persons (in judicious defiance of the observed facts) as if they were all the same kind of thing, we avoid innumerable evils. But it is not on this that we were made to live. It is idle to say that men are of equal value. If value is taken in a wordly sense – if we mean that all men are equally useful or beautiful or good or entertaining – then it is nonsense. If it means that all are of equal value as immortal souls then I think it conceals a dangerous error. The infinite value of each human soul is not a Christian doctrine. God did not die for man because of some value he perceived in him. The value of each human soul considered simply in itself, out of relation to God, is zero. As St Paul writes, to have died for valuable men would have been not divine but merely heroic; but God died for sinners. He loved us not because we were lovable, but because he is Love. It may be that he loves all equally – he certainly loved all to the death – and I

20

am not certain what the expression means. If there is equality it is in his love, not in us.

Equality is a quantitative term and therefore love often knows nothing of it. Authority exercised with humility and obedience accepted with delight are the very lines along which our spirits live. Even in the life of the affections, much more in the Body of Christ, we step outside that world which says 'I am as good as you.' It is like turning from a march to a dance. It is like taking off our clothes. We become, as Chesterton said, taller when we bow; we become lowlier when we instruct. It delights me that there should be moments in the services of my own Church when the priest stands and I kneel. As democracy becomes more complete in the outer world and opportunities for reverence are successively removed, the refreshment, the cleansing, and invigorating returns to inequality, which the Church offers us, become more and more necessary.

In this way then, the Christian life defends the single personality from the collective, not by isolating him but by giving him the status of an organ in the mystical Body. As the book of Revelation says, he is made 'a pillar in the temple of God'; and it adds, 'he shall go no more out.' That introduces a new side of our subject. That structural position in the Church which the humblest Christian occupies is eternal and even cosmic. The Church will outlive the universe; in it the individual person will outlive the universe. Everything that is joined to the immortal head will share his immortality. We hear little of this from the Christian pulpit today. What has come of our silence may be judged from the fact that recently addressing the Forces on this subject, I found that one of my audience regarded this doctrine as 'theosophical'. If we do not believe it let us be honest and relegate the Christian faith to museums. If we do, let us give up the pretence that it makes no difference. For this is the real answer to every excessive claim made by the collective. It is mortal; we shall live for ever. There will come a time when every culture, every institution, every nation, the human race, all biological life, is extinct, and every one of us is still alive. Immortality is promised to us, not to these generalities. It was not for societies or states that Christ died, but for men. In that sense Christianity must seem to secular collectivists to involve an almost frantic assertion of individuality. But then it is not the individual as such who will share Christ's victory over death. We shall share the victory by being in the Victor. A rejection, or in Scripture's strong language, a crucifixion of the natural self is the passport to everlasting life. Nothing that has not died will be resurrected. That is just how Christianity cuts across the antithesis between individualism and collectivism. There lies the maddening ambiguity of our faith as it must appear to outsiders. It sets its face relentlessly against our natural individualism; on the other hand, it gives back to those who abandon individualism an eternal possession of their own personal being, even of their bodies. As mere biological entities, each with its separate will to live and to expand, we are apparently of no account; we are cross-fodder. But as organs in the Body of Christ, as stones and pillars in the temple, we are assured of our eternal self-identity and shall live to remember the galaxies as an old tale.

This may be put in another way. Personality is eternal and inviolable. But then, personality is not a datum from which we start. The individualism in which we all begin is only a parody or shadow of it. True personality lies ahead – how far ahead, for most of us, I dare not say. And the key to it does not lie in ourselves. It will not be attained by development from within outwards. It will come to us when we occupy those places in the structure of the eternal cosmos for which we were designed or invented. As a colour first reveals its true quality when placed by an excellent artist in its pre-elected spot between certain others, as a spice reveals its true flavour when inserted just where and when a good cook wishes among the other ingredients, as the dog becomes really doggy only when he has taken his place in the household of man, so we shall then first be true persons when we have suffered ourselves to be fitted into our places. We are marble waiting to be shaped, metal waiting to be run into a mould. No doubt there are already, even in the unregenerate self, faint hints of what mould each is designed for, or what sort of pillar he will be. But it is, I think, a gross exaggeration to picture the saving of a soul as being, normally, at all like the development from seed to flower. The very words repentance, regeneration, the New Man, suggest something very different. Some tendencies in each natural man may have to be simply rejected. Our Lord speaks of eyes being plucked out and hands lopped off – a frankly Procrustean method of adaptation.

The reason we recoil from this is that we have in our day started by getting the whole picture upside down. Starting with the doctrine that every individuality is 'of infinite value' we then picture God as a kind of employment committee whose business it is to find suitable careers for souls, square holes for square pegs. In fact, however, the value of the individual does not lie in him. He is capable of receiving value. He receives it by union with Christ. There is no question of finding for him a place in the living temple which will do justice to his inherent value and give scope to his natural idiosyncrasy. The place was there first. The man was created for it. He will not be himself till he is there. We shall be true and everlasting and really divine persons only in heaven, just as we are, even now, coloured bodies only in the light.

To say this is to repeat what everyone here admits already — that we are saved by grace, that in our flesh dwells no good thing, that we are, through and through, creatures not creators, derived beings, living not of ourselves but from Christ. If I seem to have complicated a simple matter, you will, I hope, forgive me. I have been anxious to bring out two points. I have wanted to try to expel that quite un-christian worship of the human individual simply as such which is so rampant in modern thought side by side with our collectivism; for one error begets the opposite error and, far from neutralizing, they aggravate each other. I mean the pestilent notion (one sees it in literary criticism) that each of us starts with a treasure called 'personality' locked up inside him, and that to expand and express this, to guard it from interference, to be 'original', is the main end of life. This is Pelagian, or worse, and it defeats even itself. No man who values originality will ever be original. But try to tell the truth as you see it, try to do any bit of work as well as it can be done for the work's sake, and what men call originality will come unsought. Even on that level, the submission of the individual to the function is already beginning to bring true personality to birth. And secondly, I have wanted to show that Christianity is not, in the long run, concerned either with individuals or communities. Neither the individual nor the community as popular thought understands them can inherit eternal life: neither the natural self, nor the collective mass, but a new creature.

LEARNING IN WAR-TIME

A university is a society for the pursuit of learning. As students, you will be expected to make yourselves, or to start making yourselves, into what the Middle Ages called clerks: into philosophers, scientists, scholars, critics, or historians. And at first sight this seems to be an odd thing to do during a great war. What is the use of beginning a task which we have so little chance of finishing? Or, even if we ourselves should happen not to be interrupted by death or military service, why should we – indeed how can we – continue to take an interest in these placid occupations when the lives of our friends and the liberties of Europe are in the balance? Is it not like fiddling while Rome burns?

Now it seems to me that we shall not be able to answer these questions until we have put them by the side of certain other questions which every Christian ought to have asked himself in peacetime. I spoke just now of fiddling while Rome burns. But to a Christian the true tragedy of Nero must be not that he fiddled while the city was on fire but that he fiddled on the brink of hell. You must forgive me for the crude monosyllable. I know that many wiser and better Christians than I in these days do not like to mention heaven and hell even in a pulpit. I know, too, that nearly all the references to this subject in the New Testament come from a single source. But then that source is our Lord himself. People will tell you it is

St Paul, but that is untrue. These overwhelming doctrines are dominical. They are not really removable from the teaching of Christ or of his Church. If we do not believe them, our presence in this church is great tomfoolery. If we do, we must sometime overcome our spiritual prudery and mention them.

The moment we do so we can see that every Christian who comes to a university must at all times face a question compared with which the questions raised by the war are relatively unimportant. He must ask himself how it is right, or even psychologically possible, for creatures who are every moment advancing either to heaven or to hell, to spend any fraction of the little time allowed them in this world on such comparative trivialities as literature or art, mathematics or biology. If human culture can stand up to that, it can stand up to anything. To admit that we can retain our interest in learning under the shadow of these eternal issues, but not under the shadow of a European war, would be to admit that our ears are closed to the voice of reason and very wide open to the voice of our nerves and our mass emotions.

This indeed is the case with most of us: certainly with me. For that reason I think it important to try to see the present calamity in a true perspective. The war creates no absolutely new situation: it simply aggravates the permanent human situation so that we can no longer ignore it. Human life has always been lived on the edge of a precipice. Human culture has always had to exist under the shadow of something infinitely more important than itself. If men had postponed the search for knowledge and beauty until they

27

were secure, the search would never have begun. We are mistaken when we compare war with 'normal life'. Life has never been normal. Even those periods which we think most tranquil, like the nineteenth century, turn out, on closer inspection, to be full of crises, alarms, difficulties, emergencies. Plausible reasons have never been lacking for putting off all merely cultural activities until some imminent danger has been averted or some crying injustice put right. But humanity long ago chose to neglect those plausible reasons. They wanted knowledge and beauty now, and would not wait for the suitable moment that never comes. Periclean Athens leaves us not only the Parthenon but, significantly, the Funeral Oration. The insects have chosen a different line: they have sought first the material welfare and security of the hive, and presumably they have their reward. Men are different. They propound mathematical theorems in beleaguered cities, conduct metaphysical arguments in condemned cells, make jokes on scaffolds, discuss the last new poem while advancing to the walls of Quebec, and comb their hair at Thermopylae. This is not panache: it is our nature.

But since we are fallen creatures the fact that this is now our nature would not, by itself, prove that it is rational or right. We have to enquire whether there is really any legitimate place for the activities of the scholar in a world such as this. That is, we have always to answer the question: 'How can you be so frivolous and selfish as to think about anything but the salvation of human souls?' and we have, at the moment, to answer the additional question: 'How can you be so frivolous and selfish as to think of anything but the war?' Now part of our answer will be the same for both questions. The one implies that our life can, and ought, to become exclusively and explicitly religious: the other, that it can and ought to become exclusively national. I believe that our whole life can, and indeed must, become religious in a sense to be explained later. But if it is meant that all our activities are to be of the kind that can be recognized as 'sacred' and opposed to 'secular' then I would give a single reply to both my imaginary assailants. I would say, 'Whether it ought to happen or not, the thing you are recommending is not going to happen.' Before I became a Christian I do not think I fully realized that one's life, after conversion, would inevitably consist in doing most of the same things one had been doing before: one hopes, in a new spirit, but still the same things. Before I went to the last war I certainly expected that my life in the trenches would, in some mysterious sense, be all war. In fact, I found that the nearer you got to the front line the less every one spoke and thought of the allied cause and the progress of the campaign; and I am pleased to find that Tolstoy, in the greatest war book ever written, records the same thing – and so, in its own way, does the *Iliad*. Neither conversion nor enlistment in the army is really going to obliterate our human life. Christians and soldiers are still men: the infidel's idea of a religious life, and the civilian's idea of active service, are fantastic. If you attempted, in either case, to suspend your whole intellectual and aesthetic activity, you would only succeed in substituting a worse cultural life for a better.

You are not, in fact, going to read nothing, either in the Church or in the line: if you don't read good books you will read bad ones. If you don't go on thinking rationally, you will think irrationally. If you reject aesthetic satisfactions you will fall into sensual satisfactions.

There is therefore this analogy between the claims of our religion and the claims of the war: neither of them, for most of us, will simply cancel or remove from the slate the merely human life which we were leading before we entered them. But they will operate in this way for different reasons. The war will fail to absorb our whole attention because it is a finite object, and therefore intrinsically unfitted to support the whole attention of a human soul. In order to avoid misunderstanding I must here make a few distinctions. I believe our cause to be, as human causes go, very righteous, and I therefore believe it to be a duty to participate in this war. And every duty is a religious duty, and our obligation to perform every duty is therefore absolute. Thus we may have a duty to rescue a drowning man, and perhaps, if we live on a dangerous coast, to learn life-saving so as to be ready for any drowning man when he turns up. It may be our duty to lose our own lives in saving him. But if anyone devoted himself to life-saving in the sense of giving it his total attention – so that he thought and spoke of nothing else and demanded the cessation of all other human activities until everyone had learned to swim – he would be a monomaniac. The rescue of drowning men is, then, a duty worth dying for, but not worth living for. It seems to me that all political duties (among which I include military duties) are of this kind. A man may have to die for our country: but no man must, in any exclusive sense, live for his country. He who surrenders himself without reservation to the temporal claims of a nation, or a party, or a class is rendering to Caesar that which, of all things, most emphatically belongs to God: himself.

It is for a very different reason that religion cannot occupy the whole of life in the sense of excluding all our natural activities. For, of course, in some sense, it must occupy the whole of life. There is no question of a compromise between the claims of God and the claims of culture, or politics, or anything else. God's claim is infinite and inexorable. You can refuse it: or you can begin to try to grant it. There is no middle way. Yet in spite of this it is clear that Christianity does not exclude any of the ordinary human activities. St Paul tells people to get on with their jobs. He even assumes that Christians may go to dinner parties, and, what is more, dinner parties given by pagans. Our Lord attends a wedding and provides miraculous wine. Under the aegis of his Church, and in the most Christian ages, learning and the arts flourish. The solution of this paradox is, of course, well known to you. 'Whether ye eat or drink or whatsoever ye do, do all to the glory of God.'

All our merely natural activities will be accepted, if they are offered to God, even the humblest: and all of them, even the noblest, will be sinful if they are not. Christianity does not simply replace our natural life and substitute a new one: it is rather a new organization which exploits, to its own supernatural ends, these natural materials. No doubt, in a given situation, it demands the surrender of some, or of all, our merely human pursuits : it is better to be saved with one eye, than, having two, to be cast into Gehenna. But it does this, in a sense, *per accidens* – because, in those special circumstances, it has ceased to be possible to practise this or that activity to the glory of God. There is no essential quarrel between the spiritual life and the human activities as such. Thus the omnipresence of obedience to God in a Christian's life is, in a way, analogous to the omnipresence of God in space. God does not fill space as a body fills it, in the sense that parts of him are in different parts of space, excluding other objects from them. Yet he is everywhere – totally present at every point of space – according to good theologians.

We are now in a position to answer the view that human culture is an inexcusable frivolity on the part of creatures loaded with such awful responsibilities as we. I reject at once an idea which lingers in the mind of some modern people that cultural activities are in their own right spiritual and meritorious – as though scholars and poets were intrinsically more pleasing to God than scavengers and bootblacks. I think it was Matthew Arnold who first used the English word *spiritual* in the sense of the German *geistlich*, and so inaugurated this most dangerous and most anti-christian error. Let us clear it for ever from our minds. The work of a Beethoven, and the work of a char-woman, become spiritual on precisely the same condition, that of being offered to God, of being done humbly 'as to the Lord'. This does not, of course,

32

mean that it is for anyone a mere toss-up whether he should sweep rooms or compose symphonies. A mole must dig to the glory of God and a cock must crow. We are members of one body, but differentiated members, each with his own vocation. A man's upbringing, his talents, his circumstances, are usually a tolerable index of his vocation. If our parents have sent us to Oxford, if our country allows us to remain there, this is *prima facie* evidence that the life which we, at any rate, can best lead to the glory of God at present is the learned life. By leading that life to the glory of God I do not, of course, mean any attempt to make our intellectual enquiries work out to edifying conclusions. That would be, as Bacon says, to offer to the author of truth the unclean sacrifice of a lie. I mean the pursuit of knowledge and beauty, in a sense, for their own sake, but in a sense which does not exclude their being for God's sake. An appetite for these things exists in the human mind, and God makes no appetite in vain. We can therefore pursue knowledge as such, and beauty, as such, in the sure confidence that by so doing we are either advancing to the vision of God ourselves or indirectly helping others to do so. Humility, no less than the appetite, encourages us to concentrate simply on the knowledge or the beauty, not too much concerning ourselves with their ultimate relevance to the vision of God. That relevance may not be intended for us but for our betters – for men who come after and find the spiritual significance of what we dug out in blind and humble obedience to our vocation. This is the teleological argument that the existence of the impulse and the faculty prove that they must have a proper function in God's scheme — the argument by which Thomas Aquinas proves that sexuality would have existed even without the Fall. The soundness of the argument, as regards culture, is proved by experience. The intellectual life is not the only road to God, nor the safest, but we find it to be a road, and it may be the appointed road for us. Of course it will be so only so long as we keep the impulse pure and disinterested. That is the great difficulty. As the author of the *Theologia Germanica* says, we may come to love knowledge — *our* knowing — more than the thing known: to delight not in the exercise of our talents but in the fact that they are ours, or even in the reputation they bring us. Every success in the scholar's life increases this danger. If it becomes irresistible, he must give up his scholarly work. The time for plucking out the right eye has arrived.

That is the essential nature of the learned life as I see it. But it has indirect values which are especially important today. If all the world were Christian, it might not matter if all the world were uneducated. But, as it is, a cultural life will exist outside the Church whether it exists inside or not. To be ignorant and simple now — not to be able to meet the enemies on their own ground — would be to throw down our weapons, and to betray our uneducated brethren who have, under God, no defence but us against the intellectual attacks of the heathen. Good philosophy must exist, if for no other reason, because bad philosophy needs to be answered. The cool intellect must work not only against cool intellect on the other side, but against the muddy heathen mysticisms which deny intellect altogether. Most of all, perhaps, we need intimate knowledge of the past. Not that the past has any magic about it, but because we cannot study the future, and yet need something to set against the present, to remind us that the basic assumptions have been quite different in different periods and that much which seems certain to the uneducated is merely temporary fashion. A man who has lived in many places is not likely to be deceived by the local errors of his native village: the scholar has lived in many times and is therefore in some degree immune from the great cataract of nonsense that pours from the press and the microphone of his own age.

The learned life then is, for some, a duty. At the moment it looks as if it were your duty. I am well aware that there may seem to be an almost comic discrepancy between the high issues we have been considering and the immediate task you may be set down to, such as Anglo-Saxon sound laws or chemical formulæ. But there is a similar shock awaiting us in every vocation – a young priest finds himself involved in choir treats and a young subaltern in accounting for pots of jam. It is well that it should be so. It weeds out the vain, windy people and keeps in those who are both humble and tough. On that kind of difficulty we need waste no sympathy. But the peculiar difficulty imposed on you by the war is another matter: and of it I would again repeat, what I have been saying in one form or another ever since I started – do not let your nerves and emotions lead you into thinking your predicament more abnormal than it really is. Perhaps it may be useful to mention the three mental exercises

35

which may serve as defences against the three enemies which war raises up against the scholar.

The first enemy is excitement – the tendency to think and feel about the war when we had intended to think about our work. The best defence is a recognition that in this, as in everything else, the war has not really raised up a new enemy but only aggravated an old one. There are always plenty of rivals to our work. We are always falling in love or quarrelling, looking for jobs or fearing to lose them, getting ill and recovering, following public affairs. If we let ourselves, we shall always be waiting for some distraction or other to end before we can really get down to our work. The only people who achieve much are those who want knowledge so badly that they seek it while the conditions are still unfavourable. Favourable conditions never come. There are, of course, moments when the pressure of the excitement is so great that only superhuman self-control could resist it. They come both in war and peace. We must do the best we can.

The second enemy is frustration – the feeling that we shall not have time to finish. If I say to you that no one has time to finish, that the longest human life leaves a man, in any branch of learning, a beginner, I shall seem to you to be saying something quite academic and theoretical. You would be surprised if you knew how soon one begins to feel the shortness of the tether: of how many things, even in middle life, we have to say 'No time for that', 'Too late now', and 'Not for me'. But Nature herself forbids you to share that experience. A more Christian attitude, which

can be attained at any age, is that of leaving futurity
in God's hands. We may as well, for God will certainly
retain it whether we leave it to him or not. Never, in
peace or war, commit your virtue or your happiness
to the future. Happy work is best done by the man
who takes his long-term plans somewhat lightly and
works from moment to moment 'as to the Lord'. It is
only our *daily* bread that we are encouraged to ask
for. The present is the only time in which any duty
can be done or any grace received.

The third enemy is fear. War threatens us with
death and pain. No man – and specially no Christian
who remembers Gethsemane – need try to attain a
stoic indifference about these things : but we can guard
against the illusions of the imagination. We think of
the streets of Warsaw and contrast the deaths there
suffered with an abstraction called Life. But there is no
question of death or life for any of us; only a question
of this death or of that – of a machine-gun bullet now
or a cancer forty years later. What does war do to
death? It certainly does not make it more frequent :
100 per cent of us die, and the percentage cannot be
increased. It puts several deaths earlier : but I hardly
suppose that that is what we fear. Certainly when the
moment comes, it will make little difference how many
years we have behind us. Does it increase our chances
of a painful death? I doubt it. As far as I can find
out, what we call natural death is usually preceded by
suffering : and a battlefield is one of the very few
places where one has a reasonable prospect of dying
with no pain at all. Does it decrease our chances of
dying at peace with God? I cannot believe it. If active

service does not persuade a man to prepare for death, what conceivable concatenation of circumstances would? Yet war does do something to death. It forces us to remember it. The only reason why the cancer at sixty or the paralysis at seventy-five do not bother us is that we forget them. War makes death real to us: and that would have been regarded as one of its blessings by most of the great Christians of the past. They thought it good for us to be always aware of our mortality. I am inclined to think they were right. All the animal life in us, all schemes of happiness that centred in this world, were always doomed to a final frustration. In ordinary times only a wise man can realize it. Now the stupidest of us knows. We see unmistakably the sort of universe in which we have all along been living, and must come to terms with it. If we had foolish un-christian hopes about human culture, they are now shattered. If we thought we were building up a heaven on earth, if we looked for something that would turn the present world from a place of pilgrimage into a permanent city satisfying the soul of man, we are disillusioned, and not a moment too soon. But if we thought that for some souls, and at some times, the life of learning, humbly offered to God, was, in its own small way, one of the appointed approaches to the divine reality and the divine beauty which we hope to enjoy hereafter, we can think so still.

ON FORGIVENESS

We say a great many things in church (and out of church too) without thinking of what we are saying. For instance, we say in the Creed 'I believe in the forgiveness of sins.' I had been saying it for several years before I asked myself why it was in the Creed. At first sight it seems hardly worth putting in. 'If one is a Christian,' I thought, 'of course one believes in the forgiveness of sins. It goes without saying.' But the people who compiled the Creed apparently thought that this was a part of our belief which we needed to be reminded of every time we went to church. And I have begun to see that, as far as I am concerned, they were right. To believe in the forgiveness of sins is not nearly so easy as I thought. Real belief in it is the sort of thing that very easily slips away if we don't keep on polishing it up.

We believe that God forgives us our sins; but also that he will not do so unless we forgive other people their sins against us. There is no doubt about the second part of this statement. It is in the Lord's Prayer: it was emphatically stated by our Lord. If you don't forgive you will not be forgiven. No part of his teaching is clearer: and there are no exceptions to it. He doesn't say that we are to forgive other people's sins provided they are not too frightful, or provided there are extenuating circumstances, or anything of that sort. We are to forgive them all, however spiteful, however mean, however often they are repeated. If we don't, we shall be forgiven none of our own.

Now it seems to me that we often make a mistake both about God's forgiveness of our sins and about the forgiveness we are told to offer to other people's sins. Take it first about God's forgiveness. I find that when I think I am asking God to forgive me I am often in reality (unless I watch myself very carefully) asking him to do something quite different. I am asking him not to forgive me but to excuse me. But there is all the difference in the world between forgiving and excusing. Forgiveness says 'Yes, you have done this thing, but I accept your apology, I will never hold it against you and everything between us two will be exactly as it was before.' But excusing says 'I see that you couldn't help it or didn't mean it, you weren't really to blame.' If one was not really to blame then there is nothing to forgive. In that sense forgiveness and excusing are almost opposites. Of course in dozens of cases, either between God and man, or between one man and another, there may be a mixture of the two. Part of what seemed at first to be the sins turns out to be really nobody's fault and is excused; the bit that is left over is forgiven. If you had a perfect excuse you would not need forgiveness: if the whole of your action needs forgiveness then there was no excuse for it. But the trouble is that what we call 'asking God's forgiveness' very often really consists in asking God to accept our excuses. What leads us into this mistake is the fact that there usually is some amount of excuse, some 'extenuating circumstances'. We are so very anxious to point these out to God (and to ourselves) that we are apt to forget the really important thing; that is, the bit left over, the bit which the excuses don't cover, the bit which is inexcusable but not, thank God, unforgivable. And if we forget this we shall go away imagining that we have repented and been forgiven when all that has really happened is that we have satisfied ourselves with our own excuses. They may be very bad excuses: we are all too easily satisfied about ourselves.

There are two remedies for this danger. One is to remember that God knows all the real excuses very much better than we do. If there are real 'extenuating circumstances' there is no fear that he will overlook them. Often he must know many excuses that we have never thought of, and therefore humble souls will, after death, have the delightful surprise of discovering that on certain occasions they sinned much less than they had thought. All the real excusing he will do. What we have got to take to him is the inexcusable bit, the sin. We are only wasting time by talking about all the parts which can (we think) be excused. When you go to a doctor you show him the bit of you that is wrong — say, a broken arm. It would be a mere waste of time to keep on explaining that your legs and eyes and throat are all right. You may be mistaken in thinking so; and anyway, if they are really all right, the doctor will know that.

The second remedy is really and truly to believe in the forgiveness of sins. A great deal of our anxiety to make excuses comes from not really believing in it: from thinking that God will not take us to himself again unless he is satisfied that some sort of case can be made out in our favour. But that would not be forgiveness at all. Real forgiveness means looking steadily at the sin, the sin that is left over without any excuse, after all allowances have been made, and seeing it in all its horror, dirt, meanness and malice, and nevertheless being wholly reconciled to the man who has done it. That, and only that, is forgiveness; and that we can always have from God if we ask for it.

When it comes to a question of our forgiving other people, it is partly the same and partly different. It is the same because, here also, forgiving does not mean excusing. Many people seem to think it does. They think that if you ask them to forgive someone who has cheated or bullied them you are trying to make out that there was really no cheating or no bullying. But if that were so, there would be nothing to forgive. They keep on replying 'But I tell you the man broke a most solemn promise.' Exactly: that is precisely what you have to forgive. (This doesn't mean you must necessarily believe his next promise. It does mean that you must make every effort to kill every trace of resentment in your own heart – every wish to humiliate or hurt him or to pay him out.) The difference between this situation and the one in which you are asking God's forgiveness is this. In our own case we accept excuses too easily, in other people's we do not accept them easily enough. As regards my own sins it is a safe bet (though not a certainty) that the excuses are not really so good as I think: as regards other men's sins against me it is a safe bet (though not a certainty) that the excuses are better than I think. One must therefore begin by attending carefully to everything which may show that the other man was not so much to blame as we thought. But even if he is absolutely fully to blame we still have to forgive him; and even if ninety-nine per cent of his apparent guilt can be explained away by really good excuses, the problem of forgiveness begins with the one per cent of guilt which is left over. To excuse what can really produce good excuses is not Christian charity; it is only fairness. To be a Christian means to forgive the inexcusable, because God has forgiven the inexcusable in you.

This is hard. It is perhaps not so hard to forgive a single great injury. But to forgive the incessant provocations of daily life — to keep on forgiving the bossy mother-in-law, the bullying husband, the nagging wife, the selfish daughter, the deceitful son — how can we do it? Only, I think, by remembering where we stand, by meaning our words when we say in our prayers each night 'Forgive us our trespasses as we forgive those that trespass against us.' We are offered forgiveness on no other terms. To refuse it is to refuse God's mercy for ourselves. There is no hint of exceptions and God means what he says.

HISTORICISM

'He that would fly without wings must fly in his dreams.'
— Coleridge

I give the name *Historicism* to the belief that men can, by the use of their natural powers, discover an inner meaning in the historical process. I say *by the use of their natural powers* because I do not propose to deal with any man who claims to know the meaning either of all history or of some particular historical event by divine revelation. What I mean by a Historicist is a man who asks me to accept his account of the inner meaning of history on the grounds of his learning and genius. If he had asked me to accept it on the grounds that it had been shown him in a vision, that would be another matter. I should have said to him nothing. His claim (with supporting evidence in the way of sanctity and miracles) would not be for me to judge. This does not mean that I am setting up a distinction, to be applied by myself, between inspired and uninspired writers. The distinction is not between those who have and those who lack inspiration, but between those who claim and those who do not claim it. With the former I have at present no concern.

I say *an inner meaning* because I am not classifying as Historicists those who find a 'meaning' in history in any sense whatever. Thus, to find causal connections between historical events, is in my terminology the work of a historian not of a Historicist. A historian, without becoming a Historicist, may certainly infer

unknown events from known ones. He may even infer
future events from past ones; prediction may be a
folly, but it is not Historicism. He may 'interpret' the
past in the sense of reconstructing it imaginatively,
making us feel (as far as may be) what it was like, and
in that sense what it 'meant', to a man to be a twelfth-
century villein or a Roman *eques*. What makes all these
activities proper to the historian is that in them the
conclusions, like the premises, are historical. The mark
of the Historicist, on the other hand, is that he tries
to get from historical premises conclusions which are
more than historical; conclusions metaphysical or
theological or (to coin a word) atheo-logical. The
historian and the Historicist may both say that
something 'must have' happened. But *must* in the
mouth of a genuine historian will refer only to a *ratio
cognoscendi* : since A happened B 'must have' preceded it; if William the Bastard arrived in England he
'must have' crossed the sea. But 'must' in the mouth
of a Historicist can have quite a different meaning.
It may mean that events fell out as they did because
of some ultimate, transcendent necessity in the ground
of things.

When Carlyle spoke of history as a 'book of revelations' he was a Historicist. When Novalis called history
'an evangel' he was a Historicist. When Hegel saw in
history the progressive self-manifestation of absolute
spirit he was a Historicist. When a village woman says
that her wicked father-in-law's paralytic stroke is 'a
judgement on him' she is a Historicist. Evolutionism,
when it ceases to be simply a theorem in biology and
becomes a principle for interpreting the total historical

process, is a form of Historicism. Keats's *Hyperion* is
the epic of Historicism, and the words of Oceanus,

'tis the eternal law
That first in beauty should be first in might,

are as fine a specimen of Historicism as you could wish
to find.

The contention of this article is that Historicism is
an illusion and that Historicists are, at the very best,
wasting their time. I hope it is already clear that in
criticizing Historicists I am not at all criticizing
historians. It is not formally impossible that a Historicist and a historian should be the same man. But the
two characters are in fact very seldom combined.
It is usually theologians, philosophers and politicians
who become Historicists.

Historicism exists on many levels. The lowest form
of it is one that I have already mentioned: the doctrine
that our calamities (or more often our neighbours'
calamities) are 'judgements'; which here means divine
condemnations or punishments. This sort of Historicism sometimes endeavours to support itself by the
authority of the Old Testament. Some people even
talk as if it were the peculiar mark of the Hebrew
prophets to interpret history in this way. To that I
have two replies. Firstly, the Scriptures come before
me as a book claiming divine inspiration. I am not
prepared to argue with the prophets. But if any man
thinks that because God was pleased to reveal certain
calamities as 'judgements' to certain chosen persons,

he is therefore entitled to generalize and read all
calamities in the same way, I submit that this is a
non sequitur. Unless, of course, that man claims to
be himself a prophet; and then I must refer his claim
to more competent judges. But secondly, we must
insist that such an interpretation of history was not
the characteristic of ancient Hebrew religion, not the
thing which sets it apart and makes it uniquely
valuable. On the contrary, this is precisely what it
shares with popular Paganism. To attribute calamity
to the offended gods and therefore to seek out and
punish the offender, is the most natural thing in the
world and therefore the world-wide method. Examples
such as the plague in the *Iliad* [Book I] and the plague
at the opening of the *Oedipus Tyrannus* come at once
to mind. The distinctive thing, the precious peculiarity,
of Scripture is the series of divine rebuffs which this
naïve and spontaneous type of Historicism there
receives; in the whole course of Jewish history, in the
book of Job, in Isaiah's suffering servant (chapter 53),
in our Lord's answers about the disaster at Siloam
(Luke 12:4) and the man born blind (John 9:13). If
this sort of Historicism survives, it survives in spite
of Christianity. And in a vague form it certainly does
survive. Some who in general deserve to be called true
historians are betrayed into writing as if nothing failed
or succeeded that did not somehow deserve to do so.
We must guard against the emotional overtones of a
phrase like 'the judgement of history'. It might lure us
into the vulgarest of all vulgar errors, that of idolizing
as the goddess History what manlier ages belaboured

as the strumpet Fortune. That would sink us below the Christian, or even the best pagan, level. The very Vikings and Stoics knew better.

But subtler and more cultivated types of Historicism now also claim that their view is especially congenial to Christianity. It has become a commonplace, as Fr Paul Henry lately remarked in his Deneke lecture at Oxford, to say that Judaic and Christian thought are distinguished from pagan and pantheistic thought precisely by the significance which they attribute to history. For the pantheist, we are told, the content of time is simply illusion; history is a dream and salvation consists in awaking. For the Greeks, we are told, history was a mere flux or, at best, cyclic: significance was to be sought not in Becoming but in Being. For Christianity, on the other hand, history is a story with a well-defined plot, pivoted on Creation, Fall, Redemption, and Judgement. It is indeed the divine revelation *par excellence*, the revelation which includes all other revelations.

That history in a certain sense must be all this for a Christian, I do not deny. In what sense, will be explained later. For the moment, I submit that the contrast as commonly drawn between Judaic or Christian thought on the one hand and pagan or pantheistic on the other is in some measure illusory. In the modern world, quite plainly, Historicism has a pantheistic ancestor in Hegel and a materialistic progeny in the Marxists. It has proved so far a stronger weapon in our enemies' hands than in ours. If Christian Historicism is to be recommended as an

apologetic weapon it had better be recommended by
the maxim *fas est et ab hoste doceri* than on the ground
of any supposedly inherent congeniality. And if we
look at the past we shall find that the contrast works
well as between Greek and Christian but not as between Christian and other types of pagan. The Norse
gods, for example, unlike the Homeric, are beings
rooted in a historical process. Living under the shadow
of Ragnarok they are preoccupied with time. Odin is
almost the god of anxiety: in that way Wagner's
Wotan is amazingly true to the Eddaic original. In
Norse theology cosmic history is neither a cycle nor a
flux; it is irreversible, tragic epic marching deathward
to the drum-beat of omens and prophecies. And even if
we rule out Norse Paganism on the ground that it was
possibly influenced by Christianity, what shall we do
with the Romans? It is quite clear that they did not
regard history with the indifference, or with the merely
scientific or anecdotal interests, of the Greeks. They
seem to have been a nation of Historicists. I have
pointed out elsewhere that all Roman epic before Virgil
was probably metrical chronicle;[1] and the subject was
always the same – the coming-to-be of Rome. What
Virgil essentially did was to give this perennial theme
a new unity by his symbolical structure. The *Aeneid*
puts forward, though in mythical form, what is
precisely a reading of history, an attempt to show what
the *fata Jovis* were labouring to bring about. Everything is related not to Aeneas as an individual hero

[1] 'Virgil and the Subject of Secondary Epic', *A Preface to
Paradise Lost* (Oxford, 1942), pp. 32 ff.

but to Aeneas as the Rome-bearer. This, and almost
only this, gives significance to his escape from Troy,
his *amour* with Dido, his descent into Hades, and his
defeat of Turnus. *Tantae molis erat*: all history is for
Virgil an immense parturition. It is from this pagan
source that one kind of Historicism descends to Dante.
The Historicism of the *De Monarchia*, though skil-
fully, and of course sincerely, mortised into the Judaic
and Christian framework, is largely Roman and Vir-
gilian. St Augustine indeed may be rightly described
as a Christian Historicist. But it is not always remembered that he became one in order to refute pagan
Historicism. The *De Civitate* answers those who traced
the disasters of Rome to the anger of the rejected gods.
I do not mean to imply that the task was uncongenial
to St Augustine, or that his own Historicism is merely
an *argumentum ad hominem*. But it is surely absurd
to regard as specifically Christian in him the accept-
ance of a *terrain* which had in fact been chosen by the
enemy.

The close connection which some see between
Christianity and Historicism thus seems to me to be
largely an illusion. There is no *prima facie* case in its
favour on such grounds as that. We are entitled to
examine it on its merits.

What appears, on Christian premises, to be true in
the Historicist's position is this. Since all things happen
either by the divine will or at least by the divine
permission, it follows that the total content of time
must in its own nature be a revelation of God's
wisdom, justice, and mercy. In this direction we can
go as far as Carlyle or Novalis or anyone else. History

is, in that sense, a perpetual Evangel, a story written by the finger of God. If, by one miracle, the total content of time were spread out before me, and if, by another, I were able to hold all that infinity of events in my mind and if, by a third, God were pleased to comment on it so that I could understand it, then, to be sure, I could do what the Historicist says he is doing. I could read the meaning, discern the pattern. Yes; and if the sky fell we should all catch larks. The question is not what could be done under conditions never vouchsafed us *in via*, nor even (so far as I can remember) promised us *in patria*, but what can be done now under the real conditions. I do not dispute that History is a story written by the finger of God. But have we the text? (It would be dull work discussing the inspiration of the Bible if no copy of it had ever been seen on earth.)

We must remind ourselves that the word *History* has several senses. It may mean the total content of time: past, present, and future. It may mean the content of the past only, but still the total content of the past, the past as it really was in all its teeming riches. Thirdly, it may mean so much of the past as is discoverable from surviving evidence. Fourthly, it may mean so much as has been actually discovered by historians working, so to speak, 'at the face', the pioneer historians never heard of by the public, who make the actual discoveries. Fifthly, it may mean that portion, and that version, of the matter so discovered which has been worked up by great historical writers. (This is perhaps the most popular sense: *history* usually means what you read when you are reading Gibbon or Mommsen, or the Master of Trinity.[2]) Sixthly, it may mean that vague, composite picture of the past which floats, rather hazily, in the mind of the ordinary educated man.

When men say that 'History' is a revelation, or has a meaning, in which of these six senses do they use the word *History*? I am afraid that in fact they are very often thinking of history in the sixth sense; in which case their talk about revelation or meaning is surely unplausible in the extreme. For 'history' in the sixth sense is the land of shadows, the home of wraiths like Primitive Man or the Renaissance or the Ancient-Greeks-and-Romans. It is not at all surprising, of course, that those who stare at it too long should see patterns. We see pictures in the fire. The more indeterminate the object, the more it excites our mythopoeic or 'esemplastic' faculties. To the naked eye there is a face in the moon; it vanishes when you use a telescope. In the same way, the meanings or patterns discernible in 'history' (Sense Six) disappear when we turn to 'history' in any of the higher senses. They are clearest for each of us in the periods he has studied least. No one who has distinguished the different senses of the word *History* could continue to think that history (in the sixth sense) is an evangel or a revelation. It is an effect of perspective.

On the other hand, we admit that history (in Sense One) is a story written by the finger of God. Unfortunately we have not got it. The claim of the practising Historicist then will stand or fall with his

2 George Macaulay Trevelyan (1876–1962).

success in showing that history in one of the inter-
mediate senses – the first being out of reach and the
sixth useless for his purpose – is sufficiently close
to history in the first sense to share its revealing
qualities.

We drop, then, to history in Sense Two: the total
content of past time as it really was in all its richness.
This would save the Historicist if we could reasonably
believe two things: first, that the formidable omission
of the future does not conceal the point or meaning
of the story, and, secondly, that we do actually possess
history (Sense Two) up to the present moment. But
can we believe either?

It would surely be one of the luckiest things in the
world if the content of time up to the moment at which
the Historicist is writing happened to contain all that
he required for reading the significance of total
history. We ride with our backs to the engine. We have
no notion what stage in the journey we have reached.
Are we in Act I or Act V? Are our present diseases
those of childhood or senility? If, indeed, we knew
that history was cyclic we might perhaps hazard a
guess at its meaning from the fragment we have seen.
But then we have been told that the Historicists are
just the people who do not think that history is merely
cyclic. For them it is a real story with a beginning, a
middle, and an end. But a story is precisely the sort
of thing that cannot be understood till you have heard
the whole of it. Or, if there are stories (bad stories)
whose later chapters add nothing essential to their
significance, and whose significance is therefore con-

tained in something less than the whole, at least you cannot tell whether any given story belongs to that class until you have at least once read it to the end. Then, on a second reading, you may omit the dead wood in the closing chapters. I always now omit the last Book of *War and Peace*. But we have not yet read history to the end. There might be no dead wood. If it is a story written by the finger of God, there probably isn't. And if not, how can we suppose that we have seen 'the point' already? No doubt there are things we can say about this story even now. We can say it is an exciting story, or a crowded story, or a story with humorous characters in it. The one thing we must not say is what it means, or what its total pattern is.

But even if it were possible, which I deny, to see the significance of the whole from a truncated text, it remains to ask whether we have that truncated text. Do we possess even up to the present date the content of time as it really was in all its richness? Clearly not. The past, by definition, is not present. The point I am trying to make is so often slurred over by the unconcerned admission 'Of course we don't know *everything*' that I have sometimes despaired of bringing it home to other people's minds. It is not a question of failing to know everything: it is a question (at least as regards quantity) of knowing next door to nothing. Each of us finds that in his own life every moment of time is completely filled. He is bombarded every second by sensations, emotions, thoughts, which he cannot attend to for multitude, and nine-tenths of

which he must simply ignore. A single second of lived
time contains more than can be recorded. And every
second of past time has been like that for every man
that ever lived. The past (I am assuming in the
Historicist's favour that we need consider only the
human past) in its reality, was a roaring cataract of
billions upon billions of such moments: any of them
too complex to grasp in its entirety, and the aggregate
beyond all imagination. By far the greater part of this
teeming reality escaped human consciousness almost
as soon as it occurred. None of us could at this moment
give anything like a full account of his own life for the
last twenty-four hours. We have already forgotten;
even if we remembered, we have not time. The new
moments are upon us. At every tick of the clock, in
every inhabited part of the world, an unimaginable
richness and variety of 'history' falls off the world into
total oblivion. Most of the experiences in 'the past
as it really was' were instantly forgotten by the subject
himself. Of the small percentage which he remembered
(and never remembered with perfect accuracy) a
smaller percentage was ever communicated even to his
closest intimates; of this, a smaller percentage still
was recorded; of the recorded fraction only another
fraction has ever reached posterity. *Ad nos vix tenuis
famae perlabitur aura.* When once we have realized
what 'the past as it really was' means, we must freely
admit that most – that nearly all – history (in Sense
Two) is, and will remain, wholly unknown to us. And
if *per impossibile* the whole were known, it would be
wholly unmanageable. To know the whole of one

minute in Napoleon's life would require a whole
minute of your own life. You could not keep up with
it.

If these fairly obvious reflections do not trouble the
Historicist that is because he has an answer. 'Of
course,' he replies, 'I admit that we do not know and
cannot know (and, indeed, don't want to know) all the
mass of trivialities which filled the past as they fill the
present; every kiss and frown, every scratch and
sneeze, every hiccup and cough. But we know the
important facts.' Now this is a perfectly sound reply
for a historian : I am not so clear that it will do for
the Historicist. You will notice that we are now already
a long way from history in Sense One – the total story
written by the finger of God. First, we had to abandon
the parts of that story which are still in the future.
Now it appears we have not even got the text of those
parts which we call 'past'. We have only selections :
and selections which, as regards quantity, stand to the
original text as one word would stand to all the books
in the British Museum. We are asked to believe that
from selections on that scale men (not miraculously
inspired) can arrive at the meaning or plan or purport
of the original. This is credible only if it can be shown
that the selections make up in quality for what they
lack in quantity. The quality will certainly have to be
remarkably good if it is going to do that.

'The important parts of the past survive.' If a
historian says this (I am not sure that most historians
would) he means by 'importance' relevance to the
particular enquiry he has chosen. Thus, if he is an
economic historian, economic facts are for him impor-

tant: if a military historian, military facts. And he would not have embarked on his enquiry unless he had some reason for supposing that relevant evidence existed. 'Important' facts, for him, usually do survive because his undertaking was based on the probability that the facts he calls important are to be had. Sometimes he finds he was mistaken. He admits defeat and tries a new question. All this is fairly plain sailing. But the Historicist is in a different position. When he says 'Important facts survive' he must mean by the 'important' (if he is saying anything to the purpose) that which reveals the inner meaning of History. The important parts of the past must for a Hegelian Historicist be those in which Absolute Spirit progressively manifests itself; for a Christian Historicist, those which reveal the purposes of God.

In this claim I see two difficulties. The first is logical. If history is what the Historicist says – the self-manifestation of Spirit, the story written by the finger of God, the revelation which includes all other revelations – then surely he must go to history itself to teach him what is important. How does he know beforehand what sort of events are, in a higher degree than others, self-manifestations of Spirit? And if he does not know that, how does he get his assurance that it is events of that type which manage (what a convenience!) to get recorded?

The second difficulty is obvious, if we think for a moment of the process whereby a fact about the past reaches, or fails to reach, posterity. Prehistoric pottery survives because earthenware is easy to break and hard to pulverize; prehistoric poetry has perished because words, before writing, are winged. Is it reasonable to conclude either that there was no poetry or that it was, by the Historicist's standard, less important than the pottery? Is there a discovered law by which important manuscripts survive and unimportant perish? Do you ever turn out an old drawer (say, at the break-up of your father's house) without wondering at the survival of trivial documents and the disappearance of those which everyone would have thought worth preservation? And I think the real historian will allow that the actual *detritus* of the past on which he works is very much more like an old drawer than like an intelligent epitome of some longer work. Most that survives or perishes survives or perishes by chance: that is, as a result of causes which have nothing to do with either the historian's or the Historicist's interests. Doubtless, it would be possible for God so to ordain these chances that what survives is always just what the Historicist needs. But I see no evidence that he has done so; I remember no promise that he would.

The 'literary' sources, as the historian calls them, no doubt record what their writers for some reason thought important. But this is of little use unless their standards of importance were the same as God's. This seems unlikely. Their standards do not agree with one another nor with ours. They often tell us what we do not greatly want to know and omit what we think essential. It is often easy to see why. Their standard of importance can be explained by their historical situation. So, no doubt, can ours. Standards of historical importance are themselves embedded in history. But then, by what standard can we judge whether the 'important' in some high-flying Hegelian sense has survived? Have we, apart from our Christian faith, any assurance that the historical events which we regard as momentous coincide with those which would be found momentous if God showed us the whole text and deigned to comment? Why should Genghis Khan be more important than the patience or despair of some one among his victims? Might not those whom we regard as significant figures – great scholars, soldiers, and statesmen – turn out to have their chief importance as giving occasion to states of soul in individuals whom we never heard of? I do not, of course, mean that those whom we call the great are not themselves immortal souls for whom Christ died, but that in the plot of history as a whole they might be minor characters. It would not be strange if we, who have not sat through the whole play, and who have heard only tiny fragments of the scenes already played, sometimes mistook a mere supernumerary in a fine dress for one of the protagonists.

On such a small and chance selection from the total past as we have, it seems to me a waste of time to play the Historicist. The philosophy of history is a discipline for which we mortal men lack the necessary data. Nor is the attempt always a mere waste of time: it may be positively mischievous. It encourages a Mussolini to say that 'History took him by the throat' when what really took him by the throat was desire. Drivel about superior races or immanent dialectic may be used to strengthen the hand and ease the conscience of cruelty and greed. And what quack or traitor will not now woo adherents or intimidate resistance with the assurance that his scheme is inevitable, 'bound to come', and in the direction which the world is already taking?

When I have tried to explain myself on this subject in conversation I have sometimes been met by the rejoinder: 'Because historians do not know all, will you forbid them to try to understand what they do know?' But this seems to me to miss the whole point. I have already explained in what sense historians should attempt to understand the past. They may infer unknown events from known, they may reconstruct, they may even (if they insist) predict. They may, in fact, tell me almost anything they like about history except its metahistorical meaning. And the reason is surely very plain. There are enquiries in which scanty evidence is worth using. We may not be able to get certainty, but we can get probability, and half a loaf is better than no bread. But there are other enquiries in which scanty evidence has the same value as no evidence at all. In a funny anecdote, to have heard all except the last six words in which the point lies, leaves you, as a judge of its comic merits, in the same position with the man who has heard none of it. The historian seems to me to be engaged on an enquiry of the first type; the Historicist, on one of the second. But let us take a closer analogy.

Suppose a lost Greek play of which fragments totalling six lines survive. They have survived, of course, in grammarians who quoted them to illustrate rare inflexions. That is, they survive because they were important for some reason, not because they were important in the play as a play. If any one of them had dramatic importance, that is simply a lucky accident, and we know nothing about it. I do not condemn the classical scholar to produce nothing more than a bare text of the fragments any more than I condemn the historian to be a mere annalist. Let the scholar amend their corruptions and draw from them any conclusions he can about the history of Greek language, metre or religion. But let him not start talking to us about the significance of the play as a play. For that purpose the evidence before him has a value indistinguishable from zero.

The example of a defective text might be used in another way. Let us assume a mutilated manuscript, in which only a minority of passages are legible. The parts we can still read might be tolerable evidence for those features which are likely to be constant and evenly distributed over the whole; for example, spelling or handwriting. On such evidence a palaeographer might, without excessive boldness, hazard a guess about the character and nationality of the scribe. A literary critic would have much less chance of guessing correctly at the purport of the whole text. That is because the palaeographer deals with what is cyclic or recurrent, and the literary critic with something unique, and uniquely developing throughout. It is possible, though not likely, that all the torn or stained or missing leaves were written by a different scribe; and if they were not, it is very unlikely that he altered his graphic habits in all the passages we cannot check.

But there is nothing in the world to prevent the legible line (at the bottom of a page)

Erimian was the noblest of the brothers ten

having been followed on the next and now missing page, by something like

As men believed; so false are the beliefs of men.

This provides the answer to a question which may be asked: Does my canon that historical premises should yield only historical conclusions entail the corollary that scientific premises should yield only scientific conclusions? If we call the speculations of Whitehead or Jeans or Eddington 'scienticism' (as distinct from 'science') do I condemn the scienticist as much as the Historicist? I am inclined, so far as I can see my way at present, to answer No. The scientist and the historian seem to me like the palaeographer and the literary critic in my parable. The scientist studies those elements in reality which repeat themselves. The historian studies the unique. Both have a defective manuscript but its defects are by no means equally damaging to both. One specimen of gravitation, or one specimen of handwriting, for all we can see to the contrary, is as good as another. But one historical event, or one line of a poem, is different from another and different in its actual context from what it would be in any other context, and out of all these differences the unique character of the whole is built up. That is why, in my opinion, the scientist who becomes a

scienticist is in a stronger position than the historian
who becomes a Historicist. It may not be very wise to
conclude from what we know of the physical universe
that 'God is a mathematician': it seems to me, however, much wiser than to conclude anything about his
'judgements' from mere history. *Cæveas disputare de
occultis Dei judiciis*, says the author of the *Imitation*.
He even advises us what antidotes to use *quando haec
suggerit inimicus.*

It will, I hope, be understood that I am not denying
all access whatever to the revelation of God in history.
On certain great events (those embodied in the creeds)
we have what I believe to be divine comment which
makes plain so much of their significance as we need,
and can bear, to know. On other events, most of
which are in any case unknown to us, we have no such
comment. And it is also important to remember that
we all have a certain limited, but direct, access to
History in Sense One. We are allowed, indeed compelled, to read it sentence by sentence, and every
sentence is labelled *Now*. I am not, of course, referring
to what is commonly called 'contemporary history',
the content of the newspapers. That is possibly the
most phantasmal of all histories, a story written not
by the hand of God but by foreign offices, demagogues,
and reporters. I mean the real or primary history which
meets each of us moment by moment in his own
experience. It is very limited, but it is the pure, un-
edited, unexpurgated text, straight from the author's
hand. We believe that those who seek will find comment sufficient whereby to understand it in such degree
as they need; and that therefore God is every moment

'revealed in history', that is, in what MacDonald called 'the holy present'. Where, except in the present, can the Eternal be met? If I attack Historicism it is not because I intend any disrespect to primary history, the real revelation springing direct from God in every experience. It is rather because I respect this real original history too much to see with unconcern the honours due to it lavished on those fragments, copies of fragments, copies of copies of fragments, or floating reminiscences of copies of copies, which are, unhappily, confounded with it under the general name of *history*.

THE WORLD'S LAST NIGHT

There are many reasons why the modern Christian and even the modern theologian may hesitate to give to the doctrine of Christ's second coming that emphasis which was usually laid on it by our ancestors. Yet it seems to me impossible to retain in any recognizable form our belief in the divinity of Christ and the truth of the Christian revelation while abandoning, or even persistently neglecting, the promised, and threatened, return. 'He shall come again to judge the quick and the dead,' says the Apostles' Creed. 'This same Jesus,' said the angels in Acts, 'shall so come in like manner as ye have seen him go into heaven.' 'Hereafter,' said our Lord himself (by those words inviting crucifixion), 'shall ye see the Son of Man . . . coming in the clouds of heaven.' If this is not an integral part of the faith once given to the saints, I do not know what is. In the following pages I shall endeavour to deal with some of the thoughts that may deter modern men from a firm belief in, or a due attention to, the return or second coming of the Saviour. I have no claim to speak as an expert in any of the studies involved, and merely put forward the reflections which have arisen in my own mind and have seemed to me (perhaps wrongly) to be helpful. They are all submitted to the correction of wiser heads.

The grounds for modern embarrassment about this doctrine fall into two groups, which may be called the theoretical and the practical. I will deal with the theoretical first.

Many are shy of this doctrine because they are reacting (in my opinion very properly reacting) against a school of thought which is associated with the great name of Dr Albert Schweitzer. According to that school, Christ's teaching about his own return and the end of the world – what theologians call his 'apocalyptic' – was the very essence of his message. All his other doctrines radiated from it; his moral teaching everywhere presupposed a speedy end of the world. If pressed to an extreme, this view, as I think Chesterton said, amounts to seeing in Christ little more than an earlier William Miller, who created a local 'scare'. I am not saying that Dr Schweitzer pressed it to that conclusion: but it has seemed to some that his thought invites us in that direction. Hence, from fear of that extreme, arises a tendency to soft-pedal what Schweitzer's school has overemphasized.

For my own part I hate and distrust reactions not only in religion but in everything. Luther surely spoke very good sense when he compared humanity to a drunkard who, after falling off his horse on the right, falls off it next time on the left. I am convinced that those who find in Christ's apocalyptic the whole of his message are mistaken. But a thing does not vanish – it is not even discredited – because someone has spoken of it with exaggeration. It remains exactly where it was. The only difference is that if it has recently been exaggerated, we must now take special care not to overlook it; for that is the side on which the drunk man is now most likely to fall off.

The very name 'apocalyptic' assigns our Lord's

predictions of the second coming to a class. There are other specimens of it: the *Apocalypse of Baruch*, the *Book of Enoch*, or the *Ascension of Isaiah*. Christians are far from regarding such texts as Holy Scripture, and to most modern tastes the *genre* appears tedious and unedifying. Hence there arises a feeling that our Lord's predictions, being 'much the same sort of thing', are discredited. The charge against them might be put either in a harsher or a gentler form. The harsher form would run, in the mouth of an atheist, something like this: 'You see that, after all, your vaunted Jesus was really the same sort of crank or charlatan as all the other writers of apocalyptic.' The gentler form, used more probably by a modernist, would be like this: 'Every great man is partly of his own age and partly for all time. What matters in his work is always that which transcends his age, not that which he shared with a thousand forgotten contemporaries. We value Shakespeare for the glory of his language and his knowledge of the human heart, which were his own; not for his belief in witches or the divine right of kings, or his failure to take a daily bath. So with Jesus. His belief in a speedy and catastrophic end to history belongs to him not as a great teacher but as a first-century Palestinian peasant. It was one of his inevitable limitations, best forgotten. We must concentrate on what distinguished him from other first-century Palestinian peasants, on his moral and social teaching.'

As an argument against the reality of the second coming this seems to me to beg the question at issue. When we propose to ignore in a great man's teaching those doctrines which it has in common with the thought of his age, we seem to be assuming that the thought of his age was erroneous. When we select for serious consideration those doctrines which 'transcend' the thought of his own age and are 'for all time', we are assuming that the thought of *our* age is correct: for of course by thoughts which transcend the great man's age we really mean thoughts that agree with ours. Thus I value Shakespeare's picture of the transformation in old Lear more than I value his views about the divine right of kings, because I agree with Shakespeare that a man can be purified by suffering like Lear, but do not believe that kings (or any other rulers) have divine right in the sense required. When the great man's views do not seem to us erroneous we do not value them the less for having been shared with his contemporaries. Shakespeare's disdain for treachery and Christ's blessing on the poor were not alien to the outlook of their respective periods; but no one wishes to discredit them on that account. No one would reject Christ's apocalyptic on the ground that apocalyptic was common in first-century Palestine unless he had already decided that the thought of first-century Palestine was in that respect mistaken. But to have so decided is surely to have begged the question; for the question is whether the expectation of a catastrophic and divinely ordered end of the present universe is true or false.

If we have an open mind on that point, the whole problem is altered. If such an end is really going to occur, and if (as is the case) the Jews had been trained by their religion to expect it, then it is very natural that they should produce apocalyptic literature. On that view, our Lord's production of something like the other apocalyptic documents would not necessarily result from his supposed bondage to the errors of his period, but would be the divine exploitation of a sound element in contemporary Judaism; nay, the time and place in which it pleased him to be incarnate would, presumably, have been chosen because, there and then, that element existed, and had, by his eternal providence, been developed for that very purpose. For if we once accept the doctrine of the Incarnation, we must surely be very cautious in suggesting that any circumstance in the culture of first-century Palestine was a hampering or distorting influence upon his teaching. Do we suppose that the scene of God's earthly life was selected at random? — that some other scene would have served better?

But there is worse to come. 'Say what you like,' we shall be told, 'the apocalyptic beliefs of the first Christians have been proved to be false. It is clear from the New Testament that they all expected the second coming in their own lifetime. And, worse still, they had a reason, and one which you will find very embarrassing. Their Master had told them so. He shared, and indeed created, their delusion. He said in so many words, "this generation shall not pass till all these things be done." And he was wrong. He clearly knew no more about the end of the world than anyone else.'

It is certainly the most embarrassing verse in the Bible. Yet how teasing, also, that within fourteen words of it should come the statement 'But of that day and that hour knoweth no man, no, not the angels which

are in heaven, neither the Son, but the Father.' The
one exhibition of error and the one confession of
ignorance grow side by side. That they stood thus in
the mouth of Jesus himself, and were not merely
placed thus by the reporter, we surely need not doubt.
Unless the reporter were perfectly honest he would
never have recorded the confession of ignorance at all;
he could have had no motive for doing so except a
desire to tell the whole truth. And unless later copyists
were equally honest they would never have preserved
the (apparently) mistaken prediction about 'this
generation' after the passage of time had shown the
(apparent) mistake. This passage (Mark 13 : 30–2) and
the cry 'Why hast thou forsaken me?' (Mark 15 : 34)
together make up the strongest proof that the New
Testament is historically reliable. The evangelists have
the first great characteristic of honest witnesses : they
mention facts which are, at first sight, damaging to
their main contention.

The facts, then, are these : that Jesus professed
himself (in some sense) ignorant, and within a moment
showed that he really was so. To believe in the
Incarnation, to believe that he is God, makes it hard
to understand how he could be ignorant; but also
makes it certain that, if he said he could be ignorant,
then ignorant he could really be. For a God who can
be ignorant is less baffling than a God who falsely
professes ignorance. The answer of theologians is that
the God-Man was omniscient as God, and ignorant as
Man. This, no doubt, is true, though it cannot be
imagined. Nor indeed can the unconsciousness of
Christ in sleep be imagined, nor the twilight of reason

in his infancy; still less his merely organic life in his mother's womb. But the physical sciences, no less than theology, propose for our belief much that cannot be imagined.

A generation which has accepted the curvature of space need not boggle at the impossibility of imagining the consciousness of incarnate God. In that consciousness the temporal and the timeless were united. I think we can acquiesce in mystery at that point, provided we do not aggravate it by our tendency to picture the timeless life of God as, simply, another sort of time. We are committing that blunder whenever we ask how Christ could be *at the same moment* ignorant and omniscient, or how he could be the God who neither slumbers nor sleeps *while* he slept. The italicized words conceal an attempt to establish a temporal relation between his timeless life as God and the days, months, and years of his life as Man. And of course there is no such relation. The Incarnation is not an episode in the life of God: the Lamb is slain — and therefore presumably born, grown to maturity, and risen — from all eternity. The taking up into God's nature of humanity, with all its ignorance and limitations, is not itself a temporal event, though the humanity which is so taken up was, like our own, a thing living and dying in time. And if limitation, and therefore ignorance, was thus taken up, we ought to expect that the ignorance should at some time be actually displayed. It would be difficult, and, to me, repellent, to suppose that Jesus never asked a genuine question, that is, a question to which he did not know the answer. That would make of his humanity something so unlike ours

71

as scarcely to deserve the name. I find it easier to believe that when he said 'Who touched me?' (Luke 8:45) he really wanted to know.

The difficulties which I have so far discussed are, to a certain extent, debating points. They tend rather to strengthen a disbelief already based on other grounds than to create disbelief by their own force. We are now coming to something much more important and often less fully conscious. The doctrine of the second coming is deeply uncongenial to the whole evolutionary or developmental character of modern thought. We have been taught to think of the world as something that grows slowly towards perfection, something that 'progresses' or 'evolves'. Christian apocalyptic offers us no such hope. It does not even foretell (which would be more tolerable to our habits of thought) a gradual decay. It foretells a sudden, violent end imposed from without: an extinguisher popped on to the candle, a brick flung at the gramophone, a curtain rung down on the play – 'Halt!'

To this deep-seated objection I can only reply that, in my opinion, the modern conception of Progress or Evolution (as popularly imagined) is simply a myth, supported by no evidence whatever.

I say 'evolution, as popularly imagined'. I am not in the least concerned to refute Darwinism as a theorem in biology. There may be flaws in that theorem, but I have here nothing to do with them. There may be signs that biologists are already contemplating a withdrawal from the whole Darwinian position, but I claim to be no judge of such signs. It can even be argued that what

Darwin really accounted for was not the origin, but the elimination, of species, but I will not pursue that argument. For purposes of this article I am assuming that Darwinian biology is correct. What I want to point out is the illegitimate transition from the Darwinian theorem in biology to the modern myth of evolutionism or developmentalism or progress in general.

The first thing to notice is that the myth arose earlier than the theorem, in advance of all evidence. Two great works of art embody the idea of a universe in which, by some inherent necessity, the 'higher' always supersedes the 'lower'. One is Keats's *Hyperion* and the other is Wagner's *Nibelung's Ring.* And they are both earlier than the *Origin of Species.* You could not have a clearer expression of the developmental or progressive idea than Oceanus's words

> 'tis the eternal law
> That first in beauty should be first in might.

And you could not have a more ardent submission to it than those words in which Wagner describes his tetralogy.

The progress of the whole poem, therefore [he writes to Röckel in 1854], shows the necessity of recognizing and submitting to, the change, the diversity, the multiplicity, and the eternal novelty, of the Real. Wotan rises to the tragic heights of willing his own downfall. This is all that we have to learn from the history of Man – to will the Necessary, and ourselves to bring it to pass. The creative work which this highest and

73

self-renouncing will finally accomplishes is the fearless
and everloving man, Siegfried.[1]

The idea that the myth (so potent in all modern
thought) is a result of Darwin's biology would thus
seem to be unhistorical. On the contrary, the attraction
of Darwinism was that it gave to a pre-existing myth
the scientific reassurances it required. If no evidence
for evolution had been forthcoming, it would have
been necessary to invent it. The real sources of the
myth are partly political. It projects on to the cosmic
screen feelings engendered by the Revolutionary
period.

In the second place, we must notice that Darwinism
gives no support to the belief that natural selection,
working upon chance variations, has a general tendency
to produce improvement. The illusion that it has comes
from confining our attention to a few species which
have (by some possibly arbitrary standard of our own)
changed for the better. Thus the horse has improved

---

[1] '*Der Fortgang des ganzen Gedichtes zeigt demnach die
Notwendigkeit, den Wechsel, die Mannigfaltigkeit, die Vielheit,
die ewige Neuheit der Wirklichkeit und des Lebens anzuerkennen
und ihr zu weichen. Wotan schwingt sich bis zu der tragischen
Höhe, seinen Untergang zu wollen. Dies ist alles, was wir aus der
Geschichte der Menscheit zu lernen haben: das Notwendige zu
wollen und selbst zu vollbringen. Das Schöpfungswerk dieses
höchsten, selbst vernichtenden Willens ist der endlich gewonnene
furchtlose, stets liebende Mensch; Siegfried.*'
Fuller research into the origins of this potent myth would lead
us to the German idealists and thence (as I have heard suggested)
through Boehme back to Alchemy. Is the whole dialectical view
of history possibly a gigantic projection of the old dream that
we can make gold?

in the sense that *protohippos* would be less useful to us than his modern descendant. The anthropoid has improved in the sense that he now is ourselves. But a great many of the changes produced by evolution are not improvements by any conceivable standard. In battle men save their lives sometimes by advancing and sometimes by retreating. So, in the battle for survival, species save themselves sometimes by increasing, sometimes by jettisoning, their powers. There is no general law of progress in biological history.

And, thirdly, even if there were, it would not follow – it is, indeed, manifestly not the case – that there is any law of progress in ethical, cultural, and social history. No one looking at world history without some preconception in favour of progress could find in it a steady up gradient. There is often progress within a given field over a limited period. A school of pottery or painting, a moral effort in a particular direction, a practical art like sanitation or shipbuilding, may continuously improve over a number of years. If this process could spread to all departments of life and continue indefinitely, there would be 'Progress' of the sort our fathers believed in. But it never seems to do so. Either it is interrupted (by barbarian irruption or the even less resistible infiltration of modern industrialism) or else, more mysteriously, it decays. The idea which here shuts out the second coming from our minds, the idea of the world slowly ripening to perfection, is a myth, not a generalization from experience. And it is a myth which distracts us from our real duties and our real interest. It is our attempt to guess the plot of a drama in which we are the characters. But how can the characters in a play guess the plot? We are not the playwright, we are not the producer, we are not even the audience. We are on the stage. To play well the scenes in which we are 'on' concerns us much more than to guess about the scenes that follow it.

In *King Lear* (III, vii) there is a man who is such a minor character that Shakespeare has not given him even a name: he is merely 'First Servant'. All the characters around him — Regan, Cornwall, and Edmund — have fine long-term plans. They think they know how the story is going to end, and they are quite wrong. The servant has no such delusions. He has no notion how the play is going to go. But he understands the present scene. He sees an abomination (the blinding of old Gloucester) taking place. He will not stand it. His sword is out and pointed at his master's breast in a moment: then Regan stabs him dead from behind. That is his whole part: eight lines all told. But if it were real life and not a play, that is the part it would be best to have acted.

The doctrine of the second coming teaches us that we do not and cannot know when the world drama will end. The curtain may be rung down at any moment: say, before you have finished reading this paragraph. This seems to some people intolerably frustrating. So many things would be interrupted. Perhaps you were going to get married next month, perhaps you were going to get a raise next week: you may be on the verge of a great scientific discovery; you may be maturing great social and political reforms. Surely no good and wise God would be so very unreasonable as to cut all this short? Not *now*, of all moments!

But we think thus because we keep on assuming that we know the play. We do not know the play. We do not even know whether we are in Act I or Act V. We do not know who are the major and who the minor characters. The Author knows. The audience, if there is an audience (if angels and archangels and all the company of heaven fill the pit and the stalls), may have an inkling. But we, never seeing the play from outside, never meeting any characters except the tiny minority who are 'on' in the same scenes as ourselves, wholly ignorant of the future and very imperfectly informed about the past, cannot tell at what moment the end ought to come. That it will come when it ought, we may be sure; but we waste our time in guessing when that will be. That it has a meaning we may be sure, but we cannot see it. When it is over, we may be told. We are led to expect that the Author will have something to say to each of us on the part that each of us has played. The playing it well is what matters infinitely.

The doctrine of the second coming, then, is not to be rejected because it conflicts with our favourite modern mythology. It is, for that very reason, to be the more valued and made more frequently the subject of meditation. It is the medicine our condition especially needs.

And with that, I turn to the practical. There is a real difficulty in giving this doctrine the place which it ought to have in our Christian life without, at the same time, running a certain risk. The fear of that risk probably deters many teachers who accept the doctrine from saying very much about it.

We must admit at once that this doctrine has, in the past, led Christians into very great follies. Apparently many people find it difficult to believe in this great event without trying to guess its date, or even without accepting as a certainty the date that any quack or hysteric offers them. To write a history of all these exploded predictions would need a book, and a sad, sordid, tragi-comical book it would be. One such prediction was circulating when St Paul wrote his second letter to the Thessalonians. Someone had told them that 'the Day' was 'at hand'. This was apparently having the result which such predictions usually have: people were idling and playing the busybody. One of the most famous predictions was that of poor William Miller in 1843. Miller (whom I take to have been an honest fanatic) dated the second coming to the year, the day, and the very minute. A timely comet fostered the delusion. Thousands waited for the Lord at midnight on 21 March, and went home to a late breakfast on the 22nd followed by the jeers of a drunkard.

Clearly, no one wishes to say anything that will reawaken such mass hysteria. We must never speak to simple, excitable people about 'the Day' without emphasizing again and again the utter impossibility of prediction. We must try to show them that that impossibility is an essential part of the doctrine. If you do not believe our Lord's words, why do you believe in his return at all? And if you do believe them must you not put away from you, utterly and for ever, any hope of dating that return? His teaching on the subject quite clearly consisted of three propositions: (1) That he will certainly return. (2) That we cannot possibly find out when. (3) And that therefore we must always be ready for him.

Note the *therefore*. Precisely because we cannot predict the moment, we must be ready at all moments. Our Lord repeated this practical conclusion again and again; as if the promise of the return had been made for the sake of this conclusion alone. Watch, watch, is the burden of his advice. I shall come like a thief. You will not, I most solemnly assure you, you will not, see me approaching. If the householder had known at what time the burglar would arrive, he would have been ready for him. If the servant had known when his absent employer would come home, he would not have been found drunk in the kitchen. But they didn't. Nor will you. Therefore you must be ready at all times. The point is surely simple enough. The schoolboy does not know which part of his Virgil lesson he will be made to translate: that is why he must be prepared to translate *any* passage. The sentry does not know at what time an enemy will attack, or an officer inspect, his post: that is why he must keep awake *all* the time. The return is wholly unpredictable. There will be wars and rumours of wars and all kinds of catastrophes, as there always are. Things will be, in that sense, normal, the hour before the heavens roll up like a scroll. You cannot guess it. If you could, one chief purpose for which it was foretold would be frustrated. And God's purposes are not so easily frustrated as that. One's ears should be closed against any future William Miller in advance. The folly of listening to him at all is almost equal to the folly of believing him. He *couldn't* know what he pretends, or thinks, he knows.

Of this folly George MacDonald has written well. 'Do those,' he asks, 'who say, Lo here or lo there are the signs of his coming, think to be too keen for him and spy his approach? When he tells them to watch lest he find them neglecting their work, they stare this way and that, and watch lest he should succeed in coming like a thief! Obedience is the one key of life.'

The doctrine of the second coming has failed, so far as we are concerned, if it does not make us realize that at every moment of every year in our lives Donne's question 'What if this present were the world's last night?' is equally relevant.

Sometimes this question has been pressed upon our minds with the purpose of exciting fear. I do not think that is its right use. I am, indeed, far from agreeing with those who think all religious fear barbarous and degrading and demand that it should be banished from the spiritual life. Perfect love, we know, casteth out fear. But so do several other things – ignorance, alcohol, passion, presumption, and stupidity. It is very desirable that we should all advance to that perfection of love in which we shall fear no longer; but it is very undesirable, until we have reached that stage, that we should allow any inferior agent to cast out our fear. The objection to any attempt at perpetual trepidation about the second coming is, in my view, quite a different one: namely, that it will certainly not succeed.

Fear is an emotion: and it is quite impossible – even physically impossible – to maintain any emotion for very long. A perpetual excitement of hope about the second coming is impossible for the same reason. Crisis-feeling of any sort is essentially transitory. Feelings come and go, and when they come a good use can be made of them: they cannot be our regular spiritual diet.

What is important is not that we should always fear (or hope) about the End but that we should always remember, always take it into account. An analogy may help here. A man of seventy need not be always feeling (much less talking) about his approaching death: but a wise man of seventy should always take it into account. He would be foolish to embark on schemes which presuppose twenty more years of life: he would be criminally foolish not to make – indeed, not to have made long since – his will. Now, what death is to each man, the second coming is to the whole human race. We all believe, I suppose, that a man should 'sit loose' to his own individual life, should remember how short, precarious, temporary, and provisional a thing it is; should never give all his heart to anything which will end when his life ends. What modern Christians find it harder to remember is that the whole life of humanity in this world is also precarious, temporary, provisional.

Any moralist will tell you that the personal triumph of an athlete or of a girl at a ball is transitory: the point is to remember that an empire or a civilization is also transitory. All achievements and triumphs, in so far as they are merely this-worldly achievements and

triumphs, will come to nothing in the end. Most
scientists here join hands with the theologians; the
earth will not always be habitable. Man, though
longer lived than men, is equally mortal. The difference is that whereas the scientists expect only a slow
decay from within, we reckon with sudden interruption
from without – at any moment. ('What if this present
were the world's last night?')

Taken by themselves, these considerations might
seem to invite a relaxation in our efforts for the good of
posterity: but if we remember that what may be upon
us at any moment is not merely an end but a judgement, they should have no such result. They may, and
should, correct the tendency of some moderns to talk
as though duties to posterity were the only duties we
had. I can imagine no man who will look with more
horror on the End than a conscientious revolutionary
who has, in a sense sincerely, been justifying cruelties
and injustices inflicted on millions of his contemporaries by the benefits which he hopes to confer on
future generations: generations who, as one terrible
moment now reveals to him, were never going to exist.
Then he will see the massacres, the faked trials, the
deportations, to be all ineffaceably real, an essential
part, his part, in the drama that has just ended: while
the future Utopia had never been anything but a
fantasy.

Frantic administration of panaceas to the world is
certainly discouraged by the reflection that 'this
present' might be 'the world's last night'; sober work
for the future, within the limits of ordinary morality

and prudence, is not. For what comes is judgement: happy are those whom it finds labouring in their vocations, whether they were merely going out to feed the pigs or laying good plans to deliver humanity a hundred years hence from some great evil. The curtain has indeed now fallen. Those pigs will never in fact be fed, the great campaign against white slavery or governmental tyranny will never in fact proceed to victory. No matter; you were at your post when the inspection came.

Our ancestors had a habit of using the word 'judgement' in this context as if it meant simply 'punishment': hence the popular expression, 'It's a judgement on him.' I believe we can sometimes render the thing more vivid to ourselves by taking judgement in a stricter sense: not as the sentence or award, but as the verdict. Some day (and 'What if this present were the world's last night?') an absolutely correct verdict – if you like, a perfect critique – will be passed on what each of us is.

We have all encountered judgements or verdicts on ourselves in this life. Every now and then we discover what our fellow creatures really think of us. I don't of course mean what they tell us to our faces: that we usually have to discount. I am thinking of what we sometimes overhear by accident or of the opinions about us which our neighbours or employees or subordinates unknowingly reveal in their actions: and of the terrible, or lovely, judgements artlessly betrayed by children or even animals. Such discoveries can be the bitterest or sweetest experiences we have. But of course both the bitter and the sweet are limited by our doubt as to the wisdom of those who judge. We always hope that those who so clearly think us cowards or bullies are ignorant and malicious; we always fear that those who trust us or admire us are misled by partiality. I suppose the experience of the final judgement (which may break in upon us at any moment) will be like these little experiences, but magnified to the Nth.

For it will be infallible judgement. If it is favourable we shall have no fear, if unfavourable, no hope that it is wrong. We shall not only believe, we shall know, beyond doubt in every fibre of our appalled or delighted being, that as the Judge has said, so we are: neither more nor less nor other. We shall perhaps even realize that in some dim fashion we could have known it all along. We shall know and all creation will know too: our ancestors, our parents, our wives or husbands, our children. The unanswerable and (by then) self-evident truth about each will be known to all.

I do not find that pictures of physical catastrophe — that sign in the clouds, those heavens rolled up like a scroll — help one so much as the naked idea of judgement. We cannot always be excited. We can, perhaps, train ourselves to ask more and more often how the thing which we are saying or doing (or failing to do) at each moment will look when the irresistible light streams in upon it; that light which is so different from the light of this world — and yet, even now, we know just enough of it to take it into account. Women sometimes have the problem of trying to judge by artificial light how a dress will look by daylight. That is very like the problem of all of us: to dress our souls not for the electric lights of the present world but for the daylight of the next. The good dress is the one that will face that light. For that light will last longer.

RELIGION AND ROCKETRY

In my time I have heard two quite different arguments against my religion put forward in the name of science. When I was a youngster, people used to say that the universe was not only not friendly to life but positively hostile to it. Life had appeared on this planet by a millionth chance, as if at one point there had been a breakdown of the elaborate defences generally enforced against it. We should be rash to assume that such a leak had occurred more than once. Probably life was a purely terrestrial abnormality. We were alone in an infinite desert. Which just showed the absurdity of the Christian idea that there was a creator who was interested in living creatures.

But then came Professor F. B. Hoyle, the Cambridge cosmologist, and in a fortnight or so everyone I met seemed to have decided that the universe was probably quite well provided with inhabitable globes and with livestock to inhabit them. Which just showed (equally well) the absurdity of Christianity with its parochial idea that Man could be important to God.

This is a warning of what we may expect if we ever do discover animal life (vegetable does not matter) on another planet. Each new discovery, even every new theory, is held at first to have the most wide-reaching theological and philosophical consequences. It is seized by unbelievers as the basis for a new attack on Christianity; it is often, and more embarrassingly, seized by injudicious believers as the basis for a new defence.

But usually, when the popular hubbub has subsided and the novelty has been chewed over by real theologians, real scientists and real philosophers, both sides find themselves pretty much where they were before. So it was with Copernican astronomy, with Darwinism, with biblical criticism, with the new psychology. So, I cannot help expecting, it will be with the discovery of 'life on other planets' – if that discovery is ever made.

The supposed threat is clearly directed against the doctrine of the Incarnation, the belief that God of God 'for us men and for our salvation came down from heaven and was . . . made man.' Why for us men more than for others? If we find ourselves to be but one among a million races, scattered through a million spheres, how can we, without absurd arrogance, believe ourselves to have been uniquely favoured? I admit that the question could become formidable. In fact, it will become formidable when, if ever, we know the answer to five other questions.

1. Are there animals anywhere except on earth? We do not know. We do not know whether we ever shall know.

2. Supposing there were, have any of these animals what we call 'rational souls'? By this I include not merely the faculty to abstract and calculate, but the apprehension of values, the power to mean by 'good' something more than 'good for me' or even 'good for my species'. If instead of asking, 'Have they rational souls?' you prefer to ask, 'Are they spiritual animals?' I think we shall both mean pretty much the same. If the answer to either question should be No, then of

course it would not be at all strange that our species should be treated differently from theirs.

There would be no sense in offering to a creature, however clever or amiable, a gift which that creature was by its nature incapable either of desiring or of receiving. We teach our sons to read but not our dogs. The dogs prefer bones. And of course, since we do not yet know whether there are extra-terrestrial animals at all, we are a long way from knowing that they are rational (or 'spiritual').

Even if we met them we might not find it so easy to decide. It seems to me possible to suppose creatures so clever that they could talk, though they were, from the theological point of view, really only animals, capable of pursuing or enjoying only natural ends. One meets humans – the machine-minded and materialistic urban type – who *look* as if they were just that. As Christians we must believe the appearance to be false; somewhere under that glib surface there lurks, however atrophied, a human soul. But in other worlds there might be things that really are what these seem to be. Conversely, there might be creatures genuinely spiritual, whose powers of manufacture and abstract thought were so humble that we should mistake them for mere animals. God shield them from us!

3. If there are species, and rational species, other than man, are any or all of them, like us, fallen? This is the point non-Christians always seem to forget. They seem to think that the Incarnation implies some particular merit or excellence in humanity. But of course it implies just the reverse: a particular demerit and depravity. No creature that deserved Redemption

would need to be redeemed. They that are whole need not the physician. Christ died for men precisely because men are *not* worth dying for; to make them worth it. Notice what waves of utterly unwarranted hypothesis these critics of Christianity want us to swim through. We are now supposing the fall of hypothetically rational creatures whose mere existence is hypothetical!

4. If all of them (and surely *all* is a long shot) or any of them have fallen have they been denied Redemption by the Incarnation and Passion of Christ? For of course it is no very new idea that the eternal Son may, for all we know, have been incarnate in other worlds than earth and so saved other races than ours. As Alice Meynell wrote in 'Christ in the Universe':

> . . . in the eternities
> Doubtless we shall compare together, hear
> A million alien Gospels, in what guise
> He trod the Pleiades, the Lyre, the Bear.

I wouldn't go as far as 'doubtless' myself. Perhaps of all races *we* only fell. Perhaps Man is the only lost sheep; the one, therefore, whom the Shepherd came to seek. Or perhaps – but this brings us to the next wave of assumption. It is the biggest yet and will knock us head over heels, but I am fond of a tumble in the surf.

5. If we knew (which we don't) the answers to 1., 2. and 3. – and further, if we knew that Redemption by an Incarnation and Passion had been denied to creatures in need of it – is it certain that this is the

only mode of Redemption that is possible? Here of course we ask for what is not merely unknown but, unless God should reveal it, wholly unknowable. It may be that the further we were permitted to see into his councils, the more clearly we should understand that thus and not otherwise – by the birth at Bethlehem, the cross on Calvary and the empty tomb – a fallen race could be rescued. There may be a necessity for this, insurmountable, rooted in the very nature of God and the very nature of sin. But we don't know. At any rate, I don't know. Spiritual as well as physical conditions might differ widely in different worlds. There might be different sorts and different degrees of fallenness. We must surely believe that the divine charity is as fertile in recourse as it is measureless in condescension. To different diseases, or even to different patients sick with the same disease, the great Physician may have applied different remedies; remedies which we should probably not recognize as such even if we ever heard of them.

It might turn out that the redemption of other species differed from ours by working through ours. There is a hint of something like this in St Paul (Romans 8:19–23) when he says that the whole creation is longing and waiting to be delivered from some kind of slavery, and that the deliverance will occur only when we, we Christians, fully enter upon our sonship to God and exercise our 'glorious liberty'.

On the conscious level I believe that he was thinking only of our own earth: of animal, and probably vegetable, life on earth being 'renewed' or glorified at the glorification of man in Christ. But it is perhaps

90

possible – it is not necessary – to give his words a cosmic meaning. It may be that Redemption, starting with us, is to work from us and through us.

This would no doubt give man a pivotal position. But such a position need not imply any superiority in us or any favouritism in God. The general, deciding where to begin his attack, does not select the prettiest landscape or the most fertile field or the most attractive village. Christ was not born in a stable because a stable is, in itself, the most convenient or distinguished place for a maternity.

Only if we had some such function would a contact between us and such unknown races be other than a calamity. If indeed we were unfallen, it would be another matter.

It sets one dreaming – to interchange thoughts with beings whose thinking had an organic background wholly different from ours (other senses, other appetites), to be unenviously humbled by intellects possibly superior to our own yet able for that very reason to descend to our level, to descend lovingly ourselves if we met innocent and childlike creatures who could never be as strong or as clever as we, to exchange with the inhabitants of other worlds that especially keen and rich affection which exists between unlikes; it is a glorious dream. But make no mistake. It *is* a dream. We are fallen.

We know what our race does to strangers. Man destroys or enslaves every species he can. Civilized man murders, enslaves, cheats, and corrupts savage man. Even inanimate nature he turns into dust bowls and slag-heaps. There are individuals who don't. But they are not the sort who are likely to be our pioneers in space. Our ambassador to new worlds will be the needy and greedy adventurer or the ruthless technical expert. They will do as their kind has always done. What that will be if they meet things weaker than themselves, the black man and the red man can tell. If they meet things stronger, they will be, very properly, destroyed.

It is interesting to wonder how things would go if they met an unfallen race. At first, to be sure, they'd have a grand time jeering at, duping, and exploiting its innocence: but I doubt if our half-animal cunning would long be a match for godlike wisdom, selfless valour, and perfect unanimity.

I therefore fear the practical, not the theoretical, problems which will arise if ever we meet rational creatures which are not human. Against them we shall, if we can, commit all the crimes we have already committed against creatures certainly human but differing from us in features and pigmentation; and the starry heavens will become an object to which good men can look up only with feelings of intolerable guilt, agonized pity, and burning shame.

Of course after the first debauch of exploitation we shall make some belated attempt to do better. We shall perhaps send missionaries. But can even missionaries be trusted? 'Gun and gospel' have been horribly combined in the past. The missionary's holy desire to save souls has not always been kept quite distinct from the arrogant desire, the busybody's itch, to (as he calls it) 'civilize' the (as he calls them) 'natives'. Would all our missionaries recognize an unfallen race if they met it? Could they? Would they continue to press upon creatures that did not need to be saved that plan of Salvation which God has appointed to Man? Would they denounce as sins mere differences of behaviour which the spiritual and biological history of these strange creatures fully justified and which God himself had blessed? Would they try to teach those from whom they had better learn? I do not know.

What I do know is that here and now, as our only possible practical preparation for such a meeting, you and I should resolve to stand firm against all exploitation and all theological imperialism. It will not be fun. We shall be called traitors to our own species. We shall be hated of almost all men; even of some religious men. And we must not give back one single inch. We shall probably fail, but let us go down fighting for the right side. Our loyalty is due not to our species but to God. Those who are, or can become, his sons, are our real brothers even if they have shells or tusks. It is spiritual, not biological, kinship that counts.

But let us thank God that we are still very far from travel to other worlds.

I have wondered before now whether the vast astronomical distances may not be God's quarantine precautions. They prevent the spiritual infection of a fallen species from spreading. And of course we are also very far from the supposed theological problem which contact with other rational species might raise. Such species may not exist. There is not at present a shred of empirical evidence that they do. There is nothing but what the logicians would call arguments from '*a priori* probability' – arguments that begin 'It is only natural to suppose', or 'All analogy suggests', or 'Is it not the height of arrogance to rule out – ?' They make very good reading. But who except a born gambler ever risks five dollars on such grounds in ordinary life?

And, as we have seen, the mere existence of these creatures would not raise a problem. After that, we still need to know that they are fallen; then, that they have not been, or will not be, redeemed in the mode we know; and then, that no other mode is possible. I think a Christian is sitting pretty if his faith never encounters more formidable difficulties than these conjectural phantoms.

If I remember rightly, St Augustine raised a question about the theological position of satyrs, monopodes, and other semi-human creatures. He decided it would wait till we knew there were any. So can this.

'But supposing,' you say. 'Supposing all these embarrassing suppositions turned out to be true?' I can only record a conviction that they won't; a conviction which has for me become in the course of years irresistible. Christians and their opponents again and again expect that some new discovery will either turn matters of faith into matters of knowledge or else reduce them to patent absurdities. But it has never happened.

What we believe always remains intellectually possible; it never becomes intellectually compulsive. I have an idea that when this ceases to be so, the world will be ending. We have been warned that *all but* conclusive evidence against Christianity, evidence that would deceive (if it were possible) the very elect, will appear with Antichrist.

And after that there will be wholly conclusive evidence on the other side.

But not, I fancy, till then on either side.

THE EFFICACY OF PRAYER

Some years ago I got up one morning intending to have my hair cut in preparation for a visit to London, and the first letter I opened made it clear I need not go to London. So I decided to put the haircut off too. But then there began the most unaccountable little nagging in my mind, almost like a voice saying, 'Get it cut all the same. Go and get it cut.' In the end I could stand it no longer. I went. Now my barber at that time was a fellow-Christian and a man of many troubles whom my brother and I had sometimes been able to help. The moment I opened his shop door he said, 'Oh, I was praying you might come today.' And in fact if I had come a day or so later I should have been of no use to him.

It awed me; it awes me still. But of course one cannot rigorously prove a causal connection between the barber's prayers and my visit. It might be telepathy. It might be accident.

I have stood by the bedside of a woman whose thigh-bone was eaten through with cancer and who had thriving colonies of the disease in many other bones as well. It took three people to move her in bed. The doctors predicted a few months of life: the nurses (who often know better), a few weeks. A good man laid his hands on her and prayed. A year later the patient was walking (uphill, too, through rough woodland) and the man who took the last X-ray photos

96

was saying, 'These bones are as solid as rock. It's miraculous.'

But once again there is no rigorous proof. Medicine, as all true doctors admit, is not an exact science. We need not invoke the supernatural to explain the falsification of its prophecies. You need not, unless you choose, believe in a causal connection between the prayers and the recovery.

The question then arises, 'What sort of evidence would prove the efficacy of prayer?' The thing we pray for may happen, but how can you ever know it was not going to happen anyway? Even if the thing were indisputably miraculous it would not follow that the miracle had occurred because of your prayers. The answer surely is that a compulsive empirical proof such as we have in the sciences can never be attained.

Some things are proved by the unbroken uniformity of our experiences. The law of gravitation is established by the fact that, in our experience, all bodies without exception obey it. Now even if all the things that people prayed for happened, which they do not, this would not prove what Christians mean by the efficacy of prayer. For prayer is request. The essence of request, as distinct from compulsion, is that it may or may not be granted. And if an infinitely wise Being listens to the requests of finite and foolish creatures, of course he will sometimes grant and sometimes refuse them. Invariable 'success' in prayer would not prove the Christian doctrine at all. It would prove something much more like magic – a power in certain human beings to control, or compel, the course of nature.

There are, no doubt, passages in the New Testament

which may seem at first sight to promise an invariable granting of our prayers. But that cannot be what they really mean. For in the very heart of the story we meet a glaring instance to the contrary. In Gethsemane the holiest of all petitioners prayed three times that a certain cup might pass from him. It did not. After that the idea that prayer is recommended to us as a sort of infallible gimmick may be dismissed.

Other things are proved not simply by experience but by those artificially contrived experiences which we call experiments. Could this be done about prayer? I will pass over the objection that no Christian could take part in such a project, because he has been forbidden it: 'You must not try experiments on God, your Master.' Forbidden or not, is the thing even possible?

I have seen it suggested that a team of people – the more the better – should agree to pray as hard as they knew how, over a period of six weeks, for all the patients in Hospital A and none of those in Hospital B. Then you would tot up the results and see if A had more cures and fewer deaths. And I suppose you would repeat the experiment at various times and places so as to eliminate the influence of irrelevant factors.

The trouble is that I do not see how any real prayer could go on under such conditions. 'Words without thoughts never to heaven go,' says the King in *Hamlet*. Simply to say prayers is not to pray: otherwise a team of properly trained parrots would serve as well as men for our experiment. You cannot pray for the recovery of the sick unless the end you have in view is their recovery. But you can have no motive for desiring the recovery of all the patients in one hospital and none of those in another. You are not doing it in order that suffering should be relieved; you are doing it to find out what happens. The real purpose and the nominal purpose of your prayers are at variance. In other words, whatever your tongue and teeth and knees may do, you are not praying. The experiment demands an impossibility.

Empirical proof and disproof are, then, unobtainable. But this conclusion will seem less depressing if we remember that prayer is request and compare it with other specimens of the same thing.

We make requests of our fellow creatures as well as of God: we ask for the salt, we ask for a raise in pay, we ask a friend to feed the cat while we are on our holidays, we ask a woman to marry us. Sometimes we get what we ask for and sometimes not. But when we do, it is not nearly so easy as one might suppose to prove with scientific certainty a causal connection between the asking and the getting.

Your neighbour may be a humane person who would not have let your cat starve even if you had forgotten to make any arrangement. Your employer is never so likely to grant your request for a raise as when he is aware that you could get better money from a rival firm and is quite possibly intending to secure you by a raise in any case. As for the lady who consents to marry you — are you sure she had not decided to do so already? Your proposal, you know, might have been the result, not the cause, of her decision. A certain important conversation might never have taken place unless she had intended that it should.

Thus in some measure the same doubt that hangs about the causal efficacy of our prayers to God hangs also about our prayers to man. Whatever we get we might have been going to get anyway. But only, as I say, in some measure. Our friend, boss, and wife may tell us that they acted because we asked; and we may know them so well as to feel sure, first that they are saying what they believe to be true, and secondly that they understand their own motives well enough to be right. But notice that when this happens our assurance has not been gained by the methods of science. We do not try the control experiment of refusing the raise or breaking off the engagement and then making our request again under fresh conditions. Our assurance is quite different in kind from scientific knowledge. It is born out of our personal relation to the other parties; not from knowing things about them but from knowing *them*.

Our assurance – if we reach an assurance – that God always hears and sometimes grants our prayers, and that apparent grantings are not merely fortuitous, can only come in the same sort of way. There can be no question of tabulating successes and failures and trying to decide whether the successes are too numerous to be accounted for by chance. Those who best know a man best know whether, when he did what they asked, he did it because they asked. I think those who best know God will best know whether he sent me to the barber's shop because the barber prayed.

For up till now we have been tackling the whole question in the wrong way and on the wrong level.

The very question 'Does prayer work?' puts us in the wrong frame of mind from the outset. 'Work': as if it were magic, or a machine – something that functions automatically. Prayer is either a sheer illusion or a personal contact between embryonic, incomplete persons (ourselves) and the utterly concrete Person. Prayer in the sense of petition, asking for things, is a small part of it; confession and penitence are its threshold, adoration its sanctuary, the presence and vision and enjoyment of God its bread and wine. In it God shows himself to us. That he answers prayers is a corollary – not necessarily the most important one – from that revelation. What he does is learned from what he is.

Petitionary prayer is, nonetheless, both allowed and commanded to us: 'Give us our daily bread.' And no doubt it raises a theoretical problem. Can we believe that God ever really modifies his action in response to the suggestions of men? For infinite wisdom does not need telling what is best, and infinite goodness needs no urging to do it. But neither does God need any of those things that are done by finite agents, whether living or inanimate. He could, if he chose, repair our bodies miraculously without food; or give us food without the aid of farmers, bakers, and butchers; or knowledge without the aid of learned men; or convert the heathen without missionaries. Instead, he allows soils and weather and animals and the muscles, minds, and wills of men to co-operate in the execution of his will. 'God,' said Pascal, 'instituted prayer in order to lend to his creatures the dignity of causality.' But not only prayer; whenever we act at all he lends us that dignity. It is not really stranger, nor less strange, that my prayers should affect the course of events than that my other actions should do so. They have not advised or changed God's mind – that is, his over-all purpose. But that purpose will be realized in different ways according to the actions, including the prayers, of his creatures.

For he seems to do nothing of himself which he can possibly delegate to his creatures. He commands us to do slowly and blunderingly what he could do perfectly and in the twinkling of an eye. He allows us to neglect what he would have us do, or to fail. Perhaps we do not fully realize the problem, so to call it, of enabling finite free will to co-exist with Omnipotence. It seems to involve at every moment almost a sort of divine abdication. We are not mere recipients or spectators. We are either privileged to share in the game or compelled to collaborate in the work, 'to wield our little tridents'. Is this amazing process simply Creation going on before our eyes? This is how (no light matter) God makes something – indeed, makes gods – out of nothing.

So at least it seems to me. But what I have offered can be, at the very best, only a mental model or symbol. All that we say on such subjects must be merely analogical and parabolic. The reality is doubtless not comprehensible by our faculties. But we can at any rate try to expel bad analogies and bad parables. Prayer is not a machine. It is not magic. It is not advice offered to God. Our act, when we pray, must not, any more than all our other acts, be separated from the continuous act of God himself, in which alone all finite causes operate.

It would be even worse to think of those who get what they pray for as sort of court favourites, people who have influence with the throne. The refused prayer of Christ in Gethsemane is answer enough to that. And I dare not leave out the hard saying which I once heard from an experienced Christian: 'I have seen many striking answers to prayer and more than one that I thought miraculous. But they usually come at the beginning: before conversion, or soon after it. As the Christian life proceeds, they tend to be rarer. The refusals, too, are not only more frequent; they become more unmistakable, more emphatic.'

Does God then forsake just those who serve him best? Well, he who served him best of all said, near his tortured death, 'Why hast thou forsaken me?' When God becomes man, that Man, of all others, is least comforted by God, at his greatest need. There is a mystery here which, even if I had the power, I might not have the courage to explore. Meanwhile, little people like you and me, if our prayers are sometimes granted, beyond all hope and probability, had better not draw hasty conclusions to our own advantage. If we were stronger, we might be less tenderly treated. If we were braver, we might be sent, with far less help, to defend far more desperate posts in the great battle.

FERN-SEED AND ELEPHANTS

This paper arose out of a conversation I had with the Principal[1] one night last term. A book of Alec Vidler's happened to be lying on the table and I expressed my reaction to the sort of theology it contained. My reaction was a hasty and ignorant one, produced with the freedom that comes after dinner.[2] One thing led to another and before we were done I was saying a good deal more than I had meant about the type of thought which, so far as I could gather, is now dominant in many theological colleges. He then said, 'I wish you would come and say all this to my young men.' He knew of course that I was extremely ignorant of the whole thing. But I think his idea was that you ought to know how a certain sort of theology strikes the outsider. Though I may have nothing but misunderstandings to lay before you, you ought to know that such misunderstandings exist. That sort of thing is easy to overlook inside one's own circle. The minds you daily meet have been conditioned by the same studies and prevalent opinions as your own. That may

[1] The Principal of Westcott House, Cambridge, now the Bishop of Edinburgh (The Rt Rev. Kenneth Carey).

[2] While the Bishop was out of the room, Lewis read 'The Sign at Cana' in Alec Vidler's *Windsor Sermons*. The Bishop recalls that when he asked him what he thought about it, Lewis 'expressed himself very freely about the sermon and said that he thought that it was quite incredible that we should have had to wait nearly 2000 years to be told by a theologian called Vidler that what the Church has always regarded as a miracle was, in fact, a parable!'

mislead you. For of course as priests it is the outsiders you will have to cope with. You exist in the long run for no other purpose. The proper study of shepherds is sheep, not (save accidentally) other shepherds. And woe to you if you do not evangelize. I am not trying to teach my grandmother. I am a sheep, telling shepherds what only a sheep can tell them. And now I start my bleating.

There are two sorts of outsiders: the uneducated, and those who are educated in some way but not in your way. How you are to deal with the first class, if you hold views like Loisy's or Schweitzer's or Bultmann's or Tillich's or even Alec Vidler's, I simply don't know. I see – and I'm told that you see – that it would hardly do to tell them what you really believe. A theology which denies the historicity of nearly everything in the Gospels to which Christian life and affections and thought have been fastened for nearly two millennia – which either denies the miraculous altogether or, more strangely, after swallowing the camel of the Resurrection strains at such gnats as the feeding of the multitudes – if offered to the uneducated man can produce only one or other of two effects. It will make him a Roman Catholic or an atheist. What you offer him he will not recognize as Christianity. If he holds to what he calls Christianity he will leave a Church in which it is no longer taught and look for one where it is. If he agrees with your version he will no longer call himself a Christian and no longer come to church. In his crude, coarse way, he would respect you much more if you did the same. An experienced clergyman told me that most liberal priests, faced with this problem, have recalled from its grave the late medieval conception of two truths: a picture-truth which can be preached to the people, and an esoteric truth for use among the clergy. I shouldn't think you will enjoy this conception much when you have to put it into practice. I'm sure if I had to produce picture-truths to a parishioner in great anguish or under fierce temptation, and produce them with that seriousness and fervour which his condition demanded, while knowing all the time that I didn't exactly – only in some Pickwickian sense – believe them myself, I'd find my forehead getting red and damp and my collar getting tight. But that is your headache, not mine. You have, after all, a different sort of collar. I claim to belong to the second group of outsiders: educated, but not theologically educated. How one member of that group feels I must now try to tell you.

The undermining of the old orthodoxy has been mainly the work of divines engaged in New Testament criticism. The authority of experts in that discipline is the authority in deference to whom we are asked to give up a huge mass of beliefs shared in common by the early Church, the Fathers, the Middle Ages, the Reformers, and even the nineteenth century. I want to explain what it is that makes me sceptical about this authority. Ignorantly sceptical, as you will all too easily see. But the scepticism is the father of the ignorance. It is hard to persevere in a close study when you can work up no *prima facie* confidence in your teachers.

First then, whatever these men may be as Biblical critics, I distrust them as critics. They seem to me to lack literary judgement, to be imperceptive about the very quality of the texts they are reading. It sounds a strange charge to bring against men who have been steeped in those books all their lives. But that might be just the trouble. A man who has spent his youth and manhood in the minute study of New Testament texts and of other people's studies of them, whose literary experience of those texts lacks any standard of comparison such as can only grow from a wide and deep and genial experience of literature in general, is, I should think, very likely to miss the obvious things about them. If he tells me that something in a Gospel is legend or romance, I want to know how many legends and romances he has read, how well his palate is trained in detecting them by the flavour; not how many years he has spent on that Gospel. But I had better turn to examples.

In what is already a very old commentary I read that the fourth Gospel is regarded by one school as a 'spiritual romance', 'a poem not a history', to be judged by the same canons as Nathan's parable, the book of Jonah, *Paradise Lost* 'or, more exactly, *Pilgrim's Progress*'.[8] After a man has said that, why need one attend to anything else he says about any book in the world? Note that he regards *Pilgrim's Progress*, a story which professes to be a dream and flaunts its allegorical nature by every single proper name it uses, as the closest parallel. Note that the whole epic panoply of

[8] From 'The Gospel According to St John', by Walter Lock in *A New Commentary on Holy Scripture, including the Apocrypha*, ed. by Charles Gore, Henry Leighton Goudge, Alfred Guillaume (S.P.C.K., 1928), p. 241. Lock, in turn, is quoting from James Drummond's *An Inquiry into the Character and Authorship of the Fourth Gospel* (London, 1903).

Milton goes for nothing. But even if we leave out the
grosser absurdities and keep to *Jonah*, the insensitive-
ness is crass – *Jonah*, a tale with as few even pretended
historical attachments as *Job*, grotesque in incident and
surely not without a distinct, though of course edifying,
vein of typically Jewish humour. Then turn to *John*.
Read the dialogues: that with the Samaritan woman at
the well, or that which follows the healing of the man
born blind. Look at its pictures: Jesus (if I may use
the word) doodling with his finger in the dust; the
unforgettable ἦν δέ νύξ (13:30). I have been reading
poems, romances, vision-literature, legends, myths all
my life. I know what they are like. I know that not one
of them is like this. Of this text there are only two
possible views. Either this is reportage – though it may
no doubt contain errors – pretty close up to the facts;
nearly as close as Boswell. Or else, some unknown
writer in the second century, without known pre-
decessors or successors, suddenly anticipated the whole
technique of modern, novelistic, realistic narrative. If
it is untrue, it must be narrative of that kind. The
reader who doesn't see this has simply not learned to
read. I would recommend him to read Auerbach.[4]

Here, from Bultmann's *Theology of the New Testament* (p. 30) is another: 'Observe in what unassimilated fashion the prediction of the parousia (Mark
8:38) follows upon the prediction of the passion
(8:31).'[5] What can he mean? Unassimilated? Bult-

[4] Erich Auerbach's *Mimesis: The Representation of Reality in
Western Literature*, translated by Willard R. Trask (Princeton,
1953).

[5] Rudolf Bultmann, *Theology of the New Testament*, translated by Kendrick Grobel, vol. I (S.C.M. Press, 1952), p. 30.

mann believes that predictions of the parousia are older than those of the passion. He therefore wants to believe – and no doubt does believe – that when they occur in the same passage some discrepancy or 'unassimilation' must be perceptible between them. But surely he foists this on the text with shocking lack of perception. Peter has confessed Jesus to be the Anointed One. That flash of glory is hardly over before the dark prophecy begins – that the Son of Man must suffer and die. Then this contrast is repeated. Peter, raised for a moment by his confession, makes his false step; the crushing rebuff 'Get thee behind me' follows. Then, across that momentary ruin which Peter (as so often) becomes, the voice of the Master, turning to the crowd, generalizes the moral. All his followers must take up the cross. This avoidance of suffering, this self-preservation, is not what life is really about. Then, more definitely still, the summons to martyrdom. You must stand to your tackling. If you disown Christ here and now, he will disown you later. Logically, emotionally, imaginatively, the sequence is perfect. Only a Bultmann could think otherwise.

Finally, from the same Bultmann : 'The personality of Jesus has no importance for the kerygma either of Paul or of John . . . Indeed the tradition of the earliest Church did not even unconsciously preserve a picture of his personality. Every attempt to reconstruct one remains a play of subjective imagination.'[6]

So there is no personality of our Lord presented in the New Testament. Through what strange process has this learned German gone in order to make himself

[6] *Ibid.*, p. 35.

blind to what all men except him see? What evidence have we that he would recognize a personality if it were there? For it is Bultmann *contra mundum*. If anything whatever is common to all believers, and even to many unbelievers, it is the sense that in the Gospels they have met a personality. There are characters whom we know to be historical but of whom we do not feel that we have any personal knowledge — knowledge by acquaintance; such are Alexander, Attila, or William of Orange. There are others who make no claim to historical reality but whom, none the less, we know as we know real people: Falstaff, Uncle Toby, Mr Pickwick. But there are only three characters who, claiming the first sort of reality, also actually have the second. And surely everyone knows who they are: Plato's Socrates, the Jesus of the Gospels, and Boswell's Johnson. Our acquaintance with them shows itself in a dozen ways. When we look into the apocryphal gospels, we find ourselves constantly saying of this or that *logion*, 'No. It's a fine saying, but not his. That wasn't how he talked' — just as we do with all pseudo-Johnsoniana. We are not in the least perturbed by the contrasts within each character: the union in Socrates of silly and scabrous titters about Greek pederasty with the highest mystical fervour and the homeliest good sense; in Johnson, of profound gravity and melancholy with that love of fun and nonsense which Boswell never understood though Fanny Burney did; in Jesus of peasant shrewdness, intolerable severity, and irresistible tenderness. So strong is the flavour of the personality that, even while he says things which, on any other assumption than that of divine Incarnation in the fullest sense, would be appallingly arrogant, yet we – and many unbelievers too – accept him at his own valuation when he says 'I am meek and lowly of heart.' Even those passages in the New Testament which superficially, and in intention, are most concerned with the divine, and least with the human nature, bring us face to face with the personality. I am not sure that they don't do this more than any others. 'We beheld his glory, the glory as of the only begotten of the Father, full of graciousness and reality . . . which we have looked upon and our hands have handled.' What is gained by trying to evade or dissipate this shattering immediacy of personal contact by talk about 'that significance which the early Church found that it was impelled to attribute to the Master'? This hits us in the face. Not what they were impelled to do but what impelled them. I begin to fear that by *personality* Dr Bultmann means what I should call impersonality: what you'd get in a Dictionary of National Biography article or an obituary or a Victorian *Life and Letters of Yeshua Bar-Yosef* in three volumes with photographs.

That then is my first bleat. These men ask me to believe they can read between the lines of the old texts; the evidence is their obvious inability to read (in any sense worth discussing) the lines themselves. They claim to see fern-seed and can't see an elephant ten yards away in broad daylight.

Now for my second bleat. All theology of the liberal type involves at some point – and often involves throughout – the claim that the real behaviour and purpose and teaching of Christ came very rapidly to be misunderstood and misrepresented by his followers, and has been recovered or exhumed only by modern scholars. Now long before I became interested in theology I had met this kind of theory elsewhere. The tradition of Jowett still dominated the study of ancient philosophy when I was reading Greats. One was brought up to believe that the real meaning of Plato had been misunderstood by Aristotle and wildly travestied by the neo-Platonists, only to be recovered by the moderns. When recovered, it turned out (most fortunately) that Plato had really all along been an English Hegelian, rather like T. H. Green. I have met it a third time in my own professional studies; every week a clever undergraduate, every quarter a dull American don, discovers for the first time what some Shakespearian play really meant. But in this third instance I am a privileged person. The revolution in thought and sentiment which has occurred in my own lifetime is so great that I belong, mentally, to Shakespeare's world far more than to that of these recent interpreters. I see – I feel it in my bones – I know beyond argument – that most of their interpretations are merely impossible; they involve a way of looking at things which was not known in 1914, much less in the Jacobean period. This daily confirms my suspicion of the same approach to Plato or the New Testament. The idea that any man or writer should be opaque to those who lived in the same culture, spoke the same language, shared the same habitual imagery and unconscious assumptions, and yet be transparent to those who have none of these advantages, is in my opinion preposterous. There is an *a priori* improba-

bility in it which almost no argument and no evidence
could counterbalance.

Thirdly, I find in these theologians a constant use
of the principle that the miraculous does not occur.
Thus any statement put into our Lord's mouth by the
old texts, which, if he had really made it, would
constitute a prediction of the future, is taken to have
been put in after the occurrence which it seemed to
predict. This is very sensible if we start by knowing
that inspired prediction can never occur. Similarly in
general, the rejection as unhistorical of all passages
which narrate miracles is sensible if we start by knowing that the miraculous in general never occurs. Now
I do not here want to discuss whether the miraculous
is possible. I only want to point out that this is a
purely philosophical question. Scholars, as scholars,
speak on it with no more authority than anyone else.
The canon 'If miraculous, unhistorical' is one they
bring to their study of the texts, not one they have
learned from it. If one is speaking of authority, the
united authority of all the Biblical critics in the world
counts here for nothing. On this they speak simply as
men; men obviously influenced by, and perhaps in-
sufficiently critical of, the spirit of the age they grew
up in.

But my fourth bleat — which is also my loudest and
longest — is still to come.

All this sort of criticism attempts to reconstruct the
genesis of the texts it studies; what vanished documents each author used, when and where he wrote,
with what purposes, under what influences — the whole
Sitz im Leben of the text. This is done with immense

113

erudition and great ingenuity. And at first sight it is very convincing. I think I should be convinced by it myself, but that I carry about with me a charm – the herb *moly* – against it. You must excuse me if I now speak for a while of myself. The value of what I say depends on its being first-hand evidence.

What forearms me against all these reconstructions is the fact that I have seen it all from the other end of the stick. I have watched reviewers reconstructing the genesis of my own books in just this way.

Until you come to be reviewed yourself you would never believe how little of an ordinary review is taken up by criticism in the strict sense: by evaluation, praise, or censure, of the book actually written. Most of it is taken up with imaginary histories of the process by which you wrote it. The very terms which the reviewers use in praising or dispraising often imply such a history. They praise a passage as 'spontaneous' and censure another as 'laboured'; that is, they think they know that you wrote the one *currente calamo* and the other *invita Minerva*.

What the value of such reconstructions is I learned very early in my career. I had published a book of essays; and the one into which I had put most of my heart, the one I really cared about and in which I discharged a keen enthusiasm, was on William Morris.[7] And in almost the first review I was told that this was obviously the only one in the book in which I had felt no interest. Now don't mistake. The critic was, I

---

[7] 'William Morris' first appeared in *Rehabilitations* (1939) and is reprinted in Lewis's *Selected Literary Essays*, ed. Walter Hooper (1969).

now believe, quite right in thinking it the worst essay in the book; at least everyone agreed with him. Where he was totally wrong was in his imaginary history of the causes which produced its dullness.

Well, this made me prick up my ears. Since then I have watched with some care similar imaginary histories both of my own books and of books by friends whose real history I knew. Reviewers, both friendly and hostile, will dash you off such histories with great confidence; will tell you what public events had directed the author's mind to this or that, what other authors had influenced him, what his overall intention was, what sort of audience he principally addressed, why – and when – he did everything.

Now I must first record my impression; then, distinct from it, what I can say with certainty. My impression is that in the whole of my experience not one of these guesses has on any one point been right; that the method shows a record of one hundred per cent failure. You would expect that by mere chance they would hit as often as they miss. But it is my impression that they do no such thing. I can't remember a single hit. But as I have not kept a careful record my mere impression may be mistaken. What I think I can say with certainty is that they are usually wrong.

And yet they would often sound – if you didn't know the truth – extremely convincing. Many reviewers said that the Ring in Tolkien's *The Lord of the Rings* was suggested by the atom bomb. What could be more plausible? Here is a book published when everyone was preoccupied by that sinister invention; here in the centre of the book is a weapon which it seems madness to throw away yet fatal to use. Yet in fact, the chronology of the book's composition makes the theory impossible. Only the other week a reviewer said that a fairy-tale by my friend Roger Lancelyn Green was influenced by fairy-tales of mine. Nothing could be more probable. I have an imaginary country with a beneficent lion in it: Green, one with a beneficent tiger. Green and I can be proved to read one another's works; to be indeed in various ways closely associated. The case for an affiliation is far stronger than many which we accept as conclusive when dead authors are concerned. But it's all untrue nevertheless. I know the genesis of that Tiger and that Lion and they are quite independent.[8]

Now this surely ought to give us pause. The reconstruction of the history of a text, when the text is ancient, sounds very convincing. But one is after all sailing by dead reckoning; the results cannot be checked by fact. In order to decide how reliable the method is, what more could you ask for than to be

---

[8] Lewis corrected this error in the following letter, 'Books for Children', in *The Times Literary Supplement* (28 November 1958), p. 689: 'Sir,—A review of Mr R. L. Green's *Land of the Lord High Tiger* in your issue of 21 November spoke of myself (in passing) with so much kindness that I am reluctant to cavil at anything it contained: but in justice to Mr Green I must. The critic suggested that Mr Green's Tiger owed something to my fairy-tales. In reality this is not so and is chronologically impossible. The Tiger was an old inhabitant, and his land a familiar haunt, of Mr Green's imagination long before I began writing. There is a moral here for all of us as critics. I wonder how much *Quellenforschung* in our studies of older literature seems solid only because those who knew the facts are dead and can't contradict it?'

shown an instance where the same method is at work and we have facts to check it by? Well, that is what I have done. And we find, that when this check is available, the results are either always, or else nearly always, wrong. The 'assured results of modern scholarship', as to the way in which an old book was written, are 'assured', we may conclude, only because the men who knew the facts are dead and can't blow the gaff. The huge essays in my own field which reconstruct the history of *Piers Plowman* or *The Faerie Queene* are most unlikely to be anything but sheer illusions.

Am I then venturing to compare every whipster who writes a review in a modern weekly with these great scholars who have devoted their whole lives to the detailed study of the New Testament? If the former are always wrong, does it follow that the latter must fare no better?

There are two answers to this. First, while I respect the learning of the great Biblical critics, I am not yet persuaded that their judgement is equally to be respected. But, secondly, consider with what overwhelming advantages the mere reviewers start. They reconstruct the history of a book written by someone whose mother-tongue is the same as theirs; a contemporary, educated like themselves, living in something like the same mental and spiritual climate. They have everything to help them. The superiority in judgement and diligence which you are going to attribute to the Biblical critics will have to be almost superhuman if it is to offset the fact that they are everywhere faced with customs, language, race-characteristics, class-characteristics, a religious background, habits of composition, and basic assumptions, which no scholarship will ever enable any man now alive to know as surely and intimately and instinctively as the reviewer can know mine. And for the very same reason, remember, the Biblical critics, whatever reconstructions they devise, can never be crudely proved wrong. St Mark is dead. When they meet St Peter there will be more pressing matters to discuss.

You may say, of course, that such reviewers are foolish in so far as they guess how a sort of book they never wrote themselves was written by another. They assume that you wrote a story as they would try to write a story; the fact that they would so try, explains why they have not produced any stories. But are the Biblical critics in this way much better off? Dr Bultmann never wrote a gospel. Has the experience of his learned, specialized, and no doubt meritorious, life really given him any power of seeing into the minds of those long dead men who were caught up into what, on any view, must be regarded as the central religious experience of the whole human race? It is no incivility to say – he himself would admit – that he must in every way be divided from the evangelists by far more formidable barriers – spiritual as well as intellectual – than any that could exist between my reviewers and me.

My picture of one layman's reaction – and I think it is not a rare one – would be incomplete without some account of the hopes he secretly cherishes and the naïve reflections with which he sometimes keeps his spirits up.

You must face the fact he does not expect the

present school of theological thought to be everlasting. He thinks, perhaps wishfully thinks, that the whole thing may blow over. I have learned in other fields of study how transitory the 'assured results of modern scholarship' may be, how soon scholarship ceases to be modern. The confident treatment to which the New Testament is subjected is no longer applied to profane texts. There used to be English scholars who were prepared to cut up *Henry VI* between half a dozen authors and assign his share to each. We don't do that now. When I was a boy one would have been laughed at for supposing there had been a real Homer: the disintegrators seemed to have triumphed for ever. But Homer seems to be creeping back. Even the belief of the ancient Greeks that the Mycenaeans were their ancestors and spoke Greek has been surprisingly supported. We may without disgrace believe in a historical Arthur. Everywhere, except in theology, there has been a vigorous growth of scepticism about scepticism itself. We can't keep ourselves from murmuring *multa renascentur quae jam cecidere.*

Nor can a man of my age ever forget how suddenly and completely the idealist philosophy of his youth fell. McTaggart, Green, Bosanquet, Bradley seemed enthroned for ever; they went down as suddenly as the Bastille. And the interesting thing is that while I lived under that dynasty I felt various difficulties and objections which I never dared to express. They were so frightfully obvious that I felt sure they must be mere misunderstandings: the great men could not have made such very elementary mistakes as those which my objections implied. But very similar objections –

119

though put, no doubt, far more cogently than I could have put them – were among the criticisms which finally prevailed. They would now be the stock answers to English Hegelianism. If anyone present tonight has felt the same shy and tentative doubts about the great Biblical critics, perhaps he need not feel quite certain that they are only his stupidity. They may have a future he little dreams of.

We derive a little comfort, too, from our mathematical colleagues. When a critic reconstructs the genesis of a text he usually has to use what may be called linked hypotheses. Thus Bultmann says that Peter's confession is 'an Easter-story projected backward into Jesus' life-time' (p. 26, *op. cit.*). The first hypothesis is that Peter made no such confession. Then, granting that, there is a second hypothesis as to how the false story of his having done so might have grown up. Now let us suppose – what I am far from granting – that the first hypothesis has a probability of 90 per cent. Let us assume that the second hypothesis also has a probability of 90 per cent. But the two together don't still have 90 per cent, for the second comes in only on the assumption of the first. You have not A plus B; you have a complex AB. And the mathematicians tell me that AB has only an 81 per cent probability. I'm not good enough at arithmetic to work it out, but you see that if, in a complex reconstruction, you go on thus superinducing hypothesis on hypothesis, you will in the end get a complex in which, though each hypothesis by itself has in a sense a high probability, the whole has almost none.

You must not, however, paint the picture too black.

We are not fundamentalists. We think that different elements in this sort of theology have different degrees of strength. The nearer it sticks to mere textual criticism, of the old sort, Lachmann's sort, the more we are disposed to believe in it. And of course we agree that passages almost verbally identical cannot be independent. It is as we glide away from this into reconstructions of a subtler and more ambitious kind that our faith in the method wavers; and our faith in Christianity is proportionately corroborated. The sort of statement that arouses our deepest scepticism is the statement that something in a Gospel cannot be historical because it shows a theology or an ecclesiology too developed for so early a date. For this implies that we know, first of all, that there was any development in the matter, and secondly, how quickly it proceeded. It even implies an extraordinary homogeneity and continuity of development: implicitly denies that anyone could greatly have anticipated anyone else. This seems to involve knowing about a number of long dead people – for the early Christians were, after all, people – things of which I believe few of us could have given an accurate account if we had lived among them; all the forward and backward surge of discussion, preaching, and individual religious experience. I could not speak with similar confidence about the circle I have chiefly lived in myself. I could not describe the history even of my own thought as confidently as these men describe the history of the early Church's mind. And I am perfectly certain no one else could. Suppose a future scholar knew that I abandoned Christianity in my teens, and that, also in my teens, I went to an atheist tutor. Would not this seem far better evidence than most of what we have about the development of Christian theology in the first two centuries? Would he not conclude that my apostasy was due to the tutor? And then reject as 'backward projection' any story which represented me as an atheist before I went to that tutor? Yet he would be wrong. I am sorry to have become once more autobiographical. But reflection on the extreme improbability of his own life – by historical standards – seems to me a profitable exercise for everyone. It encourages a due agnosticism.

For agnosticism is, in a sense, what I am preaching. I do not wish to reduce the sceptical element in your minds. I am only suggesting that it need not be reserved exclusively for the New Testament and the Creeds. Try doubting something else.

Such scepticism might, I think, begin at the very beginning with the thought which underlies the whole demythology of our time. It was put long ago by Tyrrell. As man progresses he revolts against 'earlier and inadequate expressions of the religious idea . . . Taken literally, and not symbolically, they do not meet his need. And as long as he demands to picture to himself distinctly the term and satisfaction of that need he is doomed to doubt, for his picturings will necessarily be drawn from the world of his present experience.'[9]

In one way of course Tyrrell was saying nothing new. The Negative Theology of Pseudo-Dionysius had

[9] George Tyrrell, 'The Apocalyptic Vision of Christ' in *Christianity at the Cross-Roads* (London, 1909), p. 125.

said as much, but it drew no such conclusions as Tyrrell. Perhaps this is because the older tradition found our conceptions inadequate to God whereas Tyrrell finds it inadequate to 'the religious idea'. He doesn't say whose idea. But I am afraid he means man's idea. We, being men, know what we think: and we find the doctrines of the Resurrection, the Ascension, and the Second Coming inadequate to our thoughts. But supposing these things were the expressions of God's thought?

It might still be true that 'taken literally and not symbolically' they are inadequate. From which the conclusion commonly drawn is that they must be taken symbolically, not literally; that is, wholly symbolically. All the details are equally symbolical and analogical.

But surely there is a flaw here. The argument runs like this. All the details are derived from our present experience; but the reality transcends our experience: therefore all the details are wholly and equally symbolical. But suppose a dog were trying to form a conception of human life. All the details in its picture would be derived from canine experience. Therefore all that the dog imagined could, at best, be only analogically true of human life. The conclusion is false. If the dog visualized our scientific researches in terms of ratting, this would be analogical; but if it thought that eating could be predicated of humans only in an analogical sense, the dog would be wrong. In fact if a dog could, *per impossibile*, be plunged for a day into human life, it would be hardly more surprised by hitherto unimagined differences than by hitherto unsuspected similarities. A reverent dog would be shocked. A modernist dog, mistrusting the whole experience, would ask to be taken to the vet.

But the dog can't get into human life. Consequently, though it can be sure that its best ideas of human life are full of analogy and symbol, it could never point to any one detail and say, 'This is entirely symbolic.' You cannot know that everything in the representation of a thing is symbolical unless you have independent access to the thing and can compare it with the representation. Dr Tyrrell can tell that the story of the Ascension is inadequate to his religious idea, because he knows his own idea and can compare it with the story. But how if we are asking about a transcendent, objective reality to which the story is our sole access? 'We know not — oh we know not.' But then we must take our ignorance seriously.

Of course if 'taken literally and not symbolically' means 'taken in terms of mere physics', then this story is not even a religious story. Motion away from the earth — which is what Ascension physically means — would not in itself be an event of spiritual significance. Therefore, you argue, the spiritual reality can have nothing but an analogical connection with the story of an ascent. For the union of God with God and of man with God-man can have nothing to do with space. Who told you this? What you really mean is that we can't see how it could possibly have anything to do with it. That is a quite different proposition. When I know as I am known I shall be able to tell which parts of the story were purely symbolical and which, if any, were not; shall see how the transcendent reality either excludes and repels locality, or how unimaginably it assimilates and loads it with significance. Had we not better wait?

Such are the reactions of one bleating layman to Modern Theology. It is right you should hear them. You will not perhaps hear them very often again. Your parishioners will not often speak to you quite frankly. Once the layman was anxious to hide the fact that he believed so much less than the vicar: he now tends to hide the fact that he believes so much more. Missionary to the priests of one's own church is an embarrassing role; though I have a horrid feeling that if such mission work is not soon undertaken the future history of the Church of England is likely to be short.

Books by C. S. Lewis

The Problem of Pain

The Great Divorce

Mere Christianity

The Screwtape Letters

Screwtape Proposes a Toast

Surprised by Joy

The Four Loves

Reflections on the Psalms

Miracles

Prayer: Letters to Malcolm

Fern-seed and Elephants

Also available in Fountain Books

The Founder of Christianity
C. H. DODD

'A first-rate and fascinating book . . . This book is a theological event. It is to be unreservedly recommended and may play a powerful part in the revival of a positive and intelligent Christianity.'   *Times Literary Supplement*

The Plain Man Looks at the Bible
WILLIAM NEIL

This book is meant for the plain man who would like to know what to think about the Bible today. It deals with the relevance of the Bible and restates its message for the twentieth century.

The Bible Story
WILLIAM NEIL

'A real spiritual experience . . . written in an easy and readable style that makes it difficult to put the book down. I can think of no better way of interesting anyone in reading the Bible than by putting this book into his hands.'
R. C. Fuller, Scripture Bulletin

Companion to the Good News
J. RHYMER AND A. BULLEN

'The book admirably sums up what a beginner needs to know about the background and content of the New Testament and states the critical problems fairly.'   —

The First Christmas
H. J. RICHARDS

'Many readers will be grateful for a Biblical scholarship which gives a fresh relevance to these beautiful passages of Scripture.'
Expository Times

Also available in Fountain Books

The Boundaries of Our Being
PAUL TILLICH

Paul Tillich is generally regarded as the greatest English-speaking theologian of the twentieth century. In this volume are collected his magnificent series of sermons preached in universities and colleges between 1947 and 1963 and previously published as two books, *The New Being* and *The Eternal Now*.

The Courage To Be
PAUL TILLICH

The problem of anxiety has dominated much of contemporary literature and philosophy. In this book Paul Tillich tries to point the way toward its conquest.

Apologia Pro Vita Sua
J. H. NEWMAN

A passionate defence of Cardinal Newman's own intellectual and spiritual integrity by a man who had been under continuous attack for many years.

Newman's Journey
MERIOL TREVOR

'An exemplary life of Newman. Miss Trevor writes exceedingly well and turns the most arid of controversy to stimulus. Miss Trevor has splendidly put together the facts.' *Observer*